Those Who Come Along

Those Who Come Along

A Spiral Song of Souls

Linda R. Harrell

Phoenix TKD, Inc.

Those Who Come Along: A Spiral Song of Souls
2021 © Linda R. Harrell
ISBN 978-1-7371752-0-9

Cover drawing of Katetin and title page drawing by Aidan R. Eastman. All other drawings (except where indicated with A.E.) by Linda R. Harrell. (Readers may be interested to know that Aiden was one of the two boys in the Epilogue on page 69.) Photographs by Linda R. Harrell, except for eagle photograph on p. 74: courtesy, Avian Haven. Cover photo collage by Lindy Gifford.

Lindy Gifford, cover and book designer

Genie Dailey, editor

Title typefaces: Antiquarian and Antiquarian Scribe by 3ip.com

Phoenix TKD, Inc., publisher

To Bill Eagle
the best friend I never met

Trigger Warning

This note is included for those who have sustained trauma. My heart lies alongside yours. This applies especially to beloved Indigenous neighbors, many of whom know that I would never inflict more harm than truth asks for. I see you with the telling and do so with all the gentleness I possess. The following story includes an incident of historical violence. To tell it is to make it ring again in this time and ripple beyond itself in ever-increasing waves. It must not disappear, to happen again. A child I love wills it so.

A Teaching Story

Henry and I attained the position of Master Teachers in the Arts of Tae Kwon Do and Reiki over the last 34 years. In ancient times, this would have meant serving the larger communities in ways commensurate with our individual giftings or callings. The story we bring to you has elements of a teaching story. We suggest you read it once for enjoyment. If something catches your attention, read it again to the point of the catch and just beyond, then let it sit with you. Please allow yourself the benefit of curiosity. We find that people tell us they see more as they read it again, more insights coming with time. At the right time for each reader, understanding will happen as it is supposed to. We feel the story will tell itself to each person as Spirit has told it to us, when it is right, and when it serves to best bring people into community.   **LRH**

Acknowledgments

No one person is an island, and a journey of over half a century does, of course, include many people. Many have been tiny bright lights whose presences have been sparks of support which kept me going. Others have been more directly involved in the development of my character or provided direct support for elements of the story itself. One was a woman mentioned here in the story who was a gruff but loving older woman who has since passed. She was willing to be my mother for many years after I lost my own. For her family's sake, I will leave her name in the wind; she knows who she is. Those listed below have given permission to be mentioned directly. Others appear in the text of the story or are mentioned in addenda.

To Henry C. Harrell III, my husband and business partner in the arts, I give my thanks for your patience and perseverance in not only helping to raise my children but to expand their number with Katetin and Instip.

My journey would never be where it has arrived without my sha-manic teacher, Susan Bakaley-Marshall, MPS, ATR, and her husband and co-teacher, Dr. Chris Marshall. Susan is a wise and disciplined practitioner who has put much love and energy into the betterment of the Universe through her education and practice. She has helped me remain grounded in my practice and therefore safe. Chris has acted so as well, and has also been a gentle voice for me in a way which has been rare. Where others have pushed me to be strong, he let me know I should be cared for.

I would also like to acknowledge Lindy Gifford of Manifest Identity as my publishing consultant. She has been for three years now an early listener for the child Katetin and has continued to press for her voice to be heard once again in the larger world.

Foreword

I am Linda's husband. Born into a rationalist family in a rationalist culture, I grew up accepting as fact only that which I could see and touch. I have been a career military officer, a mathematician, and an engineer—so one for whom skepticism came naturally. Still, I was on a path that led me to be able to believe: The martial arts pursued during my teen years gave me a deep sense of and appreciation for alignment of body, mind, and spirit. In middle age, I studied Tai Chi, and the heightened sense of "chi" brought me in turn to Reiki. Working with the energy flowing through my body felt as natural as breathing. I became more fluent in the movement of energy and able to "feel" energy external to myself—and gradually it became easier to "see."

In hindsight, I see that the Universe was preparing me to be a witness to and a participant in the events described in this book, events that took place on the land by the Kennebec River. I, too, experienced the coincidences that occurred during our travels across the country; I, too, became involved with both Katetin and Instip. The emotion these two small children generated in me startled me at first, but I could not help but develop a deep love for them and a desire to help them be free of the bounds that kept them tied to this place. I became a parent of two spirit children, and once they put their small hands into mine, my heart melted and a fatherly love welled in my being. That protective nature of fatherhood bound me to them, to help in any way that I could, and embedded itself in my soul. Seeing Katetin's strength of spirit, her commitment to her brother, and her respect for her mother's wish that she stay until her mother's return, showed the breadth and depth of her culture and the core belief in family and community.

Without equivocation, my personal experience has shown me that once you begin the journey of Spirit, if you are true and honest with yourself, you cannot go back; for once you "see" them, they can "see" you.

For those that listen, Spirit calls to us to open our awareness, follow our heart, offer love, and heal the wounds inflicted by those "disconnected" from Spirit. Spirit calls us to gently show those who would continue to wound a different way to engage life and develop a Spirit-connected self. This book is an answer to that call. It is an experience of Spirit, called by purpose through time, to engage in this healing…sending its ripples through us to connect us, to heal us and be an example to others…and most of all, to *love* our brothers and sisters.

This book leads us through a fascinating journey of Spirit through time, to touch the lives of those who would see and act.

Henry Harrell

Contents

Introduction

The story that follows is a story of human souls who, for whatever reason, were meant to come together for a particular purpose. It is written for those it is meant for, at the urging of Spirit. I have been its holder, its translator, its voice, and now its author. I am asked to speak for a child no longer incarnate, about what she felt in a moment of purpose. To follow her purpose and my own, I have been helped by those named in the dedication, in the Acknowledgments, and in the silence of my heart.

If you are still with me, know that I am one of the persons who remember. At nearly sixty-four, I am grateful to be spending each of my days trying to figure out how best to fulfill the purpose to which I agreed. This story is one such attempt.

I remember part of an original set of instructions. Before I came to be here, I was elsewhere. I remember the feeling of being part of Everything That Is. Then there was a sense of being "pulled through" into separation, and a sense of aching aloneness. I was touched in my separation by Something complete and sacred and loving and I was wrapped in it. I stilled and expanded, then received an influx of memory.

It was not like watching scenes unfold. Rather, it engaged all senses in the awareness of these lifetimes. I had a sense that they were

• 1 •

mine in that they were familiar to me, but not all of me. Then came bigger scenes, less personal, some of them violent. I questioned what could be done in a situation of such violence. Once again, my soul was touched by Infinite Gentleness. I was reminded that experiences had happened to me which would prepare the way for a task and that help would be given. Then the weight of the task was given for me to hold. I felt the immensity of it in the essence of my being, and, to be honest, I shrank from it. Souls came forward and I was told they would help. I remember a soul coming forward to help me learn something hard but necessary. I could feel the weight of this soul's offer to fill this role, and a great love emerged for its willingness to do so.

The next soul who came was familiar to me in its essence. This soul had been an older man, a Peacekeeper in the world of my past experiences, which included being an Indigenous American. There was an important time coming, and I was told I might find renewed purpose following a time of great harm. I was to be a bridge, to come back to flesh to help the "Grandchildren." A sense of memory came of a great love, precious and whole which my spirit did not question. My soul reached out in acknowledgment. I was asked to do this work with the preparation and assistance given. I was not commanded or compelled. I was warned that I could not go home to this past life or use the memory of it in ways that were not of loving spirit. Despite the immensity of this idea, I reached out again for the Elder who had been a touchstone. Creator wrapped us up together and my experience of the vision ended.

The experience of "coming along" is reflected in the title of this story. To me it reflects the constant warm feeling of having a wiser presence at the soul level who accompanies the separate being of my own soul. Years ago, this presence was asked in a hypnosis session what its name was. After a long silence, it answered a name in a language familiar but not understandable to me. When later I tried to understand the term, I typed in the sound of the name: The computer identified it as "we come along" or "those who rise and come along." The language was a derivative of old Lenni Lenape or Mohegan speech. I have identified him in the Afterword as Petiseyawan. (The actual sound of this expression was closer to the older Lenni Lenape pronunciation to my ears, but in deference to the current language, it will be left as above.) As Petiseyawan states on the recording made during the session, "We circle each other… We are bound, my heart to hers; she has been part of Us before."

This lifetime has been given to me in a white, female body. In my first husband, I met the human soul who had a difficult lesson for me. At first I knew only that he was tremendously important; in later years I knew how; and in the last years of his life I remembered the burden he bore. This helped me to remember to love. His loss brought me to the next guidepost I needed to move me into an active role in my purpose: It brought me to Bill Eagle, the best friend I never met. This story is dedicated to him. *

I hope and believe there are others out there like me. Maybe one such soul will say just the right thing to just the right person and at the maximal moment in the curve of Time, with perfect precision: The critical mass of an idea will be reached and a paradigm shift will occur. This moment may look very small in the life of that single embodied soul on the day it occurs. Synchrony and perfect purpose bring this soul to the next human piece of the puzzle.

Bill Eagle taught me that my memories were possible. As a child, I

---

* See addendum "The Best Friend I Never Met."

thought everybody remembered their purpose; as a teen I discovered they didn't; and as an adult I knew safety lay in very quiet caution. Bill made these memories a precious gifting and took away my fear of them. He created space for me and my children to thrive and gave me the confidence to take a larger role in supporting the wisdom of Indigenous people. The memories I carry, as well as the time Indigenous people have gifted me, have given me clues to the nature of their wisdom; but in this body and time it is not my story or purpose to tell. If you are fortunate enough to have Indigenous people near where you live, you might respectfully seek counsel with them.

This vision never allowed me to view myself as a one-time phenomenon. This physical body arose from a family of historians, fascinated by the stories that traveled in oral folklore from Scotland, Norman France, and England. For generations, both very good and very harmful actions could be hidden, lost without trace in the passing of time. Secrets were easy to keep, those both small and personal and those that were momentous. Today, the Internet allows the people of the world to view their ancestors over hundreds of years. It's hard to disappear now, our signatures like animal tracks moving over many miles. We can view the choices our ancestors made, the alliances they kept, and the wars that cost their lives. Then, over time, we see them bound to the very people they would have considered enemies. For their children would have two heritages, or many.

And yes, I have felt anger in remembering. And regret and longing and pain. In 2013, as a gift of Spirit in shamanic journey, I was given a picture of the face of the Native man I had been. I clung to the image, not willing to give up that piece of myself. For three years I tried to let him go, unwilling to release him despite Spirit's warning. With him I was a village and home of my own. I found company in his separateness. He was a place where I could put the feelings of intensity and the racial pain that I felt for Indigenous people. It worked for me to have a secret, even as I was coming into activism on their behalf. Finally, in 2017, the wise Peacemaking soul who came along resolved this separation. This story is a part of our reunion. I now feel this soul, my former self, as a quieter and wiser presence.

This story was originally written as this Indigenous man might have spoken it, perhaps as a story in winter lodge. Time will tell how the rhythm of an oral story translates to the English written word, but that is part of the work. As a human soul, I am interested in directing the reader to a wiser source of knowledge: that of Indigenous wisdom. I think of myself still as a good second, as the subordinate my former self would have been to an older, wiser force. I do not ask the reader to believe me. My starting position is to ask you to believe that I believe: Having lived this personal truth for these many years, I have at least the persistence of vision. If you would like to learn more, please read on.

Linda R. Harrell

Earthwalk

Linda's Song

At first there was a sense of motion like flying: a sense of freedom in its purest form. And then there was a spark, like the touch of a fingertip or a bloom of color. It was more a feeling than a thought. Afterwards, somehow I knew I was perfectly unique in my own right, loved and whole. I had purpose and the right of all beings to live and have joy. I would touch the feeling in dreams occasionally in childhood, as if I was a bright bloom in a field of flowers, all unique in close-up vision, but all shining with a larger light and seen from farther off, like a network of stars.

The slice of lemon-colored light widened as the door to a darkened room swung wider. With stealth born of troubled nights, the warm presence of the woman came closer, carrying a rain smell of freshly washed hair and skin. She observed the child in the crib with an ironic smile. Did this long-awaited child never sleep?

Quiet reserve was the expression on that tiny face. Dark-blue, nearly violet eyes shifted to hers, tiny drafts blowing wispy curls across her still face. Try as she might, Anne could not recall seeing fright or surprise cross the child's face. Neither did she seem able to catch her sleeping without becoming the focus of that quiet gaze. What does she think of? Not that she missed the tears and temper her friends warned of, though she occasionally wondered if all was well. The child seemed untroubled and complete: "She's all of a piece" on her own, the mother decided. Sometimes she would hear the small girl sing quietly, as if pulling in notes from another time; but if she stuck her head in to speak, the little one's song would end and reserve would shutter her small face again.

Eventually, as these things happen, her first child was joined by a dark-haired, spirited sister. Anne's worry about the elder's quiet was buried beneath the climbing, running, busy demands of a younger child. As feisty as the other was silent, the younger of the two moved quickly, often requiring and demanding rescue with outraged complaints of injustice. They could be seen together, the smaller enclosed in the embrace of the elder, her small frame temporarily rendered still by her sister's arms. And so it went for some time, until the elder was six and the younger four. Nights began to change then, when the elder began to leave her bed at night, first to walk and then to run.

My first memories aside, the ones I recall the best involved my mother. She was slender and dark, reminiscent of the Pictish people who were her ancestors from Scotland and Wales. She had olive skin, chestnut hair, and warm hazel eyes. In appearance she was about as different from my red-gold coloring as two persons could be. At night she would hold me close to her skin and stand me on her lap as if to solve a mystery, staring deep into my small personhood.

In the quiet of the nights, I remember feeling confused about how I had come to occupy such a small, helpless space. It was as if the essence of me understood who I was and why I came to be here, and yet the words to relate this had escaped me. I loved the small dark woman who came to visit. She assured me of our kinship in her touch and acceptance of what she saw in me, although she seemed foreign on some accounts. My worries were soothed in the warmth of her arms and the softness of her breasts. When my small sister was born, I once again turned inside myself. The beloved woman seemed to have a job for me to do. "Where is your sister?" she frequently queried. And, over time, the mission and vision I had come with began to fade until it seemed only a dream.

Katetin's Song

The impact of the cannonball sent splinters of bark and dirt clods flying as a shrill whistle rent the air. Katetin folded into herself just before a hollow *whump!* of impact passed through her thin chest and down her spine. Breathless, she kept her hands over her head, dropping to her knees. New leaves and catkins floated down from the tree line overhead, and the smell of spring winds combined with hints of last winter's leaf mold. Her mind kept threatening to drift off into shock, over-focusing on some elements of her surroundings and fading others. A patch of white blossoming bloodroot captured her attention. Thoughts slowed, and it seemed all she could see was the way the broad leaves wrapped around the slender stem, like a warm shawl protecting the fragile blossom above. Then the association hit and Katetin remembered her mother's last words: "Stay here, Katetin, protect your brothers until I come for you." Ratcheting her head around and clearing the dirt from her face, she could see fire through mist and smoke. Running figures had converged near the height of land. A wagon pulled by a dark-colored horse seemed to be the focus of the activity, the horse straining to escape both wagon and harness as the four-pound balls continued to whistle about the hillside.

Katetin briefly glimpsed the breadth of her father's shoulders as he struggled with a strangely dressed opponent for something in the cart. The horse broke free, its mane alight in the reflection of sun on smoke. Then the dark horse was running, and goosebumps rose on Katetin's arms. Where were the other children? Where were her brothers?

Linda's Song

Anne's older child began to walk at night. By the time she was six, she would leave her bed, quickly traveling the length of the house and down the stairs. Her parents would follow along, smiling at her and at each other. They would ask her questions as she busily poked her head into each room along the hall. "Watcha doin', Lin?" they'd ask her. "Looking," she would chirp. It became a game for them to quiz her each night. She would walk along, sound asleep, and, while the focus of the child's search changed, she was always searching. Sometimes she would singsong a chant or chirp to an imaginary cat, which she would then dutifully let outside. Her actions seemed harmless enough. She would always return to bed and did not seem afraid. Just a phase, they decided.

As happens for all children, my memories ceased to be part of my parents' stories and became my own. By the time I was eight, I began to run. Rising bolt upright from the top nest of a bunk bed, I would scramble over my sister's bed, occasionally falling. Screams would ricochet down the hall as I ran. When I ran headfirst into a closet door, they called a doctor. Waking me seemed to make the problem worse. For my parents, it became an ordeal every two or three nights: the panicked runs in unwakeable sleep. I remember the chase through the dark and the smell of smoke. I would try to climb their frames as they desperately held me tight. By day there was no memory. My parents knew me as quiet and sweet. Now and again the doctors spoke of night terrors. They assumed it would pass along with whatever troubled me.

That same year, there was an incident which seemed to worsen the dreams. During a game of neighborhood children playing at John Wayne, older children directed younger friends to choose up for "cowboys and Indians." "Who wants to be a cowboy?" the oldest queried. In dress-up boots and hat, he cut a fine figure. "Me, me!" yelled most of the younger children. "Who wants to be an Indian?" Two children responded, including myself. I smiled, remembering the scenes from the movies my dad watched so fondly: the way the men had seemed to be a part of the mountains they flowed from, and a part of the horses they sat.

When the sides lined up, it was easy to see the difference in numbers. When the game became a battle and the blows began to fall in earnest, I could not understand. "This is what happens to Indians!" the head cowboy yelled. My parents found me some hours later a neighborhood away, with no idea how I got there or where I was. They were frantic and angry. Through their fear, I was punished again.

I had little memory for several days. That time has a hazy feel, and I still do not have the memory of it. Gradually, things returned to normal. The preteens were spoken to at the insistence of my parents, but I was no longer allowed to play. Our family moved to a quieter place outside of town, but the runs continued—only now I would awaken outside. By this time, though, I was able to tell my parents that I ran from a black horse chasing, its mane on fire and the light of the fire reflected in its black, bulging eyes.

Separation

Portent

The Jesuit priests at Sillery had much work to do. It was late April, in the year of our Lord 1638. For some time, there had been missions into the vast wilderness called New France by the French King (the area later to be named the State of Maine). The purpose of the missions was the religious conversion of its Native inhabitants. Trade had begun as well, starting an avalanche of First Blood outbreaks that devastated much of the Native population in a tiny span of time.

Because of the virulent and sudden outbreaks, the healers had little time to consider which of the Green Beings accompanying the settlers might be used to stop the ravaging of the Native people's immune systems, since nothing in the local landscape seemed to slow the devastation and there was no time to adjust. With the first wave of deaths a part of the region's history for over two decades, the Jesuits began to travel the waters of the interior. This had been discussed among the Native elders at the last fall council fires and at winter camp. It had been a long winter season with much snow, but the discipline of the hunters and the skill of the gatherers had kept all fed and warm through the slow spring thaw. Grandmother had drawn Katetin and her brother close for many stories about Gluscabe and the beginning of the world, until her lungs failed and the damp chill took her from them in the early spring.

Because of the depth of the cold, the pelts Katetin's father brought for trade were sleek and fat. Conditions had been right for a bountiful fall, with the production of millions of acorns and nuts. Parasites were few, and the herds had wintered the deep snow unusually well. At eight, Katetin was her mother's right hand in the care of her two small brothers. Although Katetin would miss her Grandmother's quiet wisdom, another small soul had come in the form of a tiny baby brother. Her first brother, Instip, at age five was no longer a toddler and was now able to spend small amounts of time with the men. At once brave and sweet, he seemed a child caught in two worlds: no longer willing to cleave to the women's group, but not quite ready to abandon the comfort and company of his sister. Adventures were undertaken with varying degrees of success. If the results were messy or frightening, she would see his stocky frame headed to her with grim determination. Not quite ready to let him go, she would gently wipe his face with a soft skin. And for a small moment, it was easy to think that things might not have to change.

But Katetin's father knew that change already had a larger hold on the People; the awareness of it floated between the words of the Elders. It whispered among the carefully chosen words of the hunters. Like smoke from the fire, it wove soft ropes between the men and women. "Death comes," it confided. "The medicine is failing," it shared. For all had heard of the sickness that came to the villages, some quite soon after contact with the new people, some like lightning strikes continuing to spread months after contact. The medawlinno spoke breath to the Green Beings, but the adder's strike of disease was unpredictable. The warriors felt the sickness had the quality of a weapon, hidden perhaps behind the doors of ships and houses to use at will. Katetin's father understood the feeling this engendered, but felt the truth was yet unseen and must be better understood. Some spoke of the White Eyes' new God, and the power of their people not to succumb to the sickness. So when it came to pass that a man like themselves was to speak on the Long Snake (Kennebis or Kennebec River), Katetin's father grudgingly agreed to make a study of the situation. It was said that this distant relative had studied among the black-robed Jesuits in the north.

Katetin's mother smiled in quick excitement. The trading village on the Kennebis was not far from where the speaker would appear. Her work with the beautiful hides this winter would surely bring in some of the trade items the women discussed. Katetin was now old enough to help manage the small boys. With a man and three young children to feed, she could use the conveniences which might make up for the loss of Grandmother's help.

Katetin's father was not as sure the trade would be simple. For some time now, the focus of trade had moved northwest to the home of the Huron, where the press of contact with White settlers was not as fierce. For the ancient people living between the northern and eastern rivers, food was becoming more scarce and resources less attainable. He feared that convenience kept the bands longer in one place than in years past. With food less available, some were finding it harder to return to traditional life. Life was also harsh for the families of White settlers at its northern border, and tempers had occasionally erupted into outright conflict. In the Great Sickenings of the previous two decades, Native people had succumbed to malnutrition added to the devastation of disease. It was said that in the Land of the Grandfathers whole villages had simply disappeared, wigwams found silent and eerily still. From the Native side, there was no need of direct contact. Livestock wandering in from the homesteads were perhaps not just trampling the gardens: Illness seemed to appear just from their presence. There was a great deal to consider in this visit to the trading post, enough that it seemed to the quiet man that his thoughts were like rolling pebbles: all movement and little resolution. He decided to make the visit to hear the words for himself and bask for a time in the beauty of his wife's smile.

And so it came to be that the small band led by Katetin's father and uncle crossed the Kennebec at a low ford and made their way downriver on its higher western bank. The father established a campsite at a small bend overlooking the river. This allowed the view of the river, both upstream and downriver to the proposed speaking site, to be within his sight, with the trader's concourse at Cushnoc in the far distance. Here was a gradual slope out of harm's way, with a small watercourse and a commanding view of the river's southern exposure. At his back would be the old road leading to Narantsouak, a quiet blending back into the obscurity of the woods should he decide it was prudent.

Katetin's family was soon joined by two more, both including relatives from her mother's family. With shelters completed and food for the evening meal in preparation, Katetin had time to notice the changes a year had brought to the younger members of her kin. Two nearly teenaged boys had become helpful additions to the young hunters and engaged Instip with his small practice bow, using their leggy frames to simulate deer as the younger boy drew determined aim. Katetin and two older girls raced across the meadow, hiding from each other and playing at a game of ring-pin. Hiding the circlets from each other, each child tried to be the first to find small areas of disturbance, then to spear each ring with their pins of wood. They traced their way down the gentle slope toward the expanse of oaks and maples which lined the river's edge. Predominant among them stood an ancient oak surrounded by thickets of hawthorn and beech. Katetin stopped short, her attention drawn to the oak's massive arms, raised as if in supplication. She had seen her mother and aunts assume the same position as the sun cleared the eastern hills. Their people were Chkuwabonikiyiq: "The People Who Live in the Land Where the Sun First Looks Their Way." And, being so seen, they must be the first to express their joy in the morning's blessings.

In thinking so, Katetin's attention was drawn to the base of the great Tree, where ironwood formed a dense, dark base; then higher, to the thorn pattern of hawthorn not yet in bloom. Raindrops clung to each leaf bud and slender branch like tears. In a heartbeat, the setting sun struck each globe, setting the tree afire with a million lights. The wind gusted, and each drop shivered and danced. From the center rose a

Hummingbird, arcing upward. It paused before the girls. As they stared in amazement, its wings lengthened and formed two dark eyes in the whiskered, mischievous face of Otter. "Who are You?" they breathed. As if in response, the eyes shifted upward into a graceful, antlered rack above the dark eyes of a magnificent deer. "I am the Spirit of this Place," breathed the Wind. Seconds later it was gone. Sun dropped behind the western hills and light swept upward, leaving the girls in hushed, dark silence.

Katetin's spirit soared on the way back to camp. The girls dispersed, each to find someone with whom to share their story. The men and elders had gathered for council fire, the women circulating among them with plates of venison. Katetin searched the group for Grandmother, before remembering their loss. The emergence of Spirit into the normalcy of routine made her suddenly exhausted. Spying a rare opportunity, she climbed into her father's arms and rested her head against the curve of his shoulder. Talk was of the next day's travel to the trader's camp downriver, and Katetin fell asleep to the sound of their low, rhythmic voices.

The family's journey several miles into Cushnoc began the next morning after only a bit more discussion by the men. After some thought, it was decided that Katetin's uncle would accompany her father and their family to the trading post. There had been a tension between the traders and Native fur owners for several years now; the presence of British settlers had caused a northern contraction in the trade. Markets on the more southern rivers had become tighter, and tempers had flared when outside marketers had tried to bypass those who had become dependent on the fur trade for survival.

Katetin's father spoke softly to his brother-in-law as the earthfast buildings of the post came into view through the trees.

With his wife interested in the trade of the furs and the perusing of the post's shelves of goods and supplies, another set of eyes on the small children seemed advisable. The men moved the family forward, noting the strong flow of the tidal current. Gusty puffs of wind moved upriver from the south, feeling like smoke from Grandfather's pipe. The two men glanced at each other and grinned, remembering the figures they had seen bloom in the smoke of the winter lodge in years before. Their next steps were frozen by a shrill shriek, drawing their attention to a small group gathered at the rear of one of the buildings. Cool water ran in rivulets down the split-shingle roof to patter in unpredictable patterns on passersby below. Under the eaves was a group of men in their early twenties, loosely surrounding a young woman of similar age. A predictable amount of tussle and bravado had led to the young woman being jostled into the path of the frigid drops, as the young men's competition for her attention became more boisterous.

Katetin's father weighed the encounter and partially dismissed it. Part of his mind, however, noted that the group seemed to stand apart, interacting little with the remainder of the post's visitors and traders. The largely middle-aged traders seemed to wave and nod to those they found familiar, their tones occasionally jesting but otherwise serious.

Then the family was through the door of the main building, the trailing ends of the travois of furs lifting and settling into the hard dirt floor. Katetin's mother's eyes threatened to swallow her small oval face as she took in the contents of the shelves in the midst of swirling dust motes. It was dark in the interior of the building compared to the bright spring sun outside. They passed rows and shelves of metal pots and knives, bins of hand-forged nails, shot, and flints. They stepped in front of ceramic goods from far away, and pipes of every sort. The rich and musky smell of tobacco formed a counterpoint to the aroma of damp wood, moss, and old decay. It was then that Katetin saw it, amongst the goods from France and Spain and nestled next to a Turkish pipe. It was a tiny hand drum, two-sided, with hide strips and beaded ends. The twin heads were covered with taut skin and gaily painted red and yellow. The circular assemblage was made to be held between a child's palms. Each twist would cause the hanging strips to strike the twin heads in a rhythmic pattern. At about the same time, Katetin noticed Instip's intense regard for a tiny wooden carving, that of a three-inch-tall pileated woodpecker. It had been carefully painted, its tiny head ablaze with a scarlet crest. This was May-May, a beloved figure from Grandmother's tales, a friend to the People. Their mother smiled, bending to indicate her approval of the children's choices. Carefully considering the weight and beauty of the season's winter furs, she was certain there would be enough for her anticipated cookpot, axe blade, and small things for her children's joy. Little enough time for them to be small, and Katetin already so serious, she thought.

During these times, things were less simple. A glut of furs had passed through Canada late this winter, aided by Kanien'keha'ka (Mohawk) and Wyandot (Huron) competitors, and tension among Kennebec traders had heightened precipitately. Just as precipitately, they had had to drop the reimbursement price for southern furs. When Katetin's father and uncle approached the weary-eyed merchant, he swept a hand through graying hair and told them the recompense would be much lower. Communication was only partially adequate. When Katetin's mother approached, she felt there was a question of the quality, and fearing the children's and her own disappointment, she became upset. She had prepared the hides herself, and ran her hand over the soft furs to show their suppleness. When their price was again refused, her mind jumped to an incident some years earlier, when a White island trader had met a bad end after repeatedly cheating a Native family two days downriver. Katetin could not clearly understand the exchange, but her mother's rigid posture told a story she understood.

Wearied by too many such encounters and faced with the prospect of yet another family's need, the tradesman signaled the finality of the discussion. He was not unkind, but he was straddling a fine line between survival and loss where a trader's communication did not suffice. From the layman's perspective, there was no guidebook on how to handle the fragile accord where cultures met and retracted, and they had not understood each other's intent. For each group found themselves participants in a survival game where the rules were political and constantly shifting.

Katetin's mother led the family out as the men dropped back to discuss the impact of the encounter. Instip's understanding of economics and protocol did not include leaving the wooden bird behind, and his rigid resistance was equaled only by his grief and unhappiness. As the distance increased, his disbelief rose to top volume. Around the corner the women came, trying to lift the distraught child onto the travois. As she turned to take him from her mother, Katetin didn't notice the group of young men from the outskirts of the post as they joined her mother. Surrounding the mother and children in a loose knot, they signaled a willingness to make an offer for the unsold furs. Astounded to be approached by unmarried males of a different race, the mother struggled both to retain composure and understand what they asked. Surely, they indicated, some money was better than none, and they knew a trader downriver who might take them. Declining politely by her gestures, she tried to withdraw from the negotiation, looking past the youths to observe whether her husband and brother had caught up. As she turned to hand her infant to Katetin and take over the struggling toddler, one man gestured toward her as if to help. There, amidst looks and taunts from the other young males, he took the handle of the travois and the others closed around it.

Katetin's mother was not an uncomplicated soul. As the wife of a band leader with her own status, she was gentle but well able to stand her own ground. As she faced down the group of men, she did not miss the poor care of their clothing or the subtle threat of desperation that lent an edge to the tone of their jesting. Placing the children behind her, she stepped back and drew herself up. Mistaking this for weakness and with their vanguard lined out in front, the youth who had approached her placed himself between the grips of the travois and backed away. The others closed the gap in front. As a single body, they turned to follow their leader until the fir branches closed behind them and they were gone.

Then the family stood alone in disbelief. Two settler women came around the corner and behind them followed Katetin's father and uncle. In the span of a very few minutes, they had discussed the likelihood of finding a different trade partner and decided to come back without the family as time permitted. When his eyes met the shocked gaze of his wife, her confusion and embarrassment turned to anger. The couple spoke none of it, however, in the presence of the strange women, although Katetin's face was a collage of fleeting and conflicting emotion. As his vision swung between them and noticed the missing furs, his pace quickened and the truth became evident. He remembered his feeling that the group he'd noted as outsiders earlier did not belong here. They were opportunists willing to approach an older married woman directly, and the result was evident. But with the children in tow, there would be no pursuit that day. For better or worse, return to camp to consider their options was the only answer. And they would do it without a winter's worth of furs.

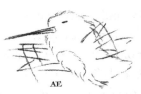

AE

Linda's Song

The glass felt cool as my head rested against the windowsill; fat May raindrops rolled across the pane. The window faced the woods beyond the backyard, and was enclosed in an overgrown lilac bush. The first clusters of fat flowers had already bloomed, and their scent came to me with the rain. Peonies drooped with their burden of drops beneath the clothesline where my mother, Anne, hung the family's clothes. At nearly fourteen, I had shaken off the social awkwardness of two moves before settling two years in Maine. Since then my father and I had grown closer. We hunted and fished, and I was allowed time off from school to be part of the men's hunts. Now that I was active and included, the nightmares stopped. I painted and danced, and friendships became easy. There was time to nap and dream.

My head leaning on the glass, I was seeing again a powerful dream I had recently had. I began to realize its connection to the "cowboys and Indians" incident from so many years before. In my mind, the days followed on each other fairly normally. Following that incident, I had not been allowed contact with the older children, but did befriend a small boy of the same age. This child had been unknown to me in all my wanderings previously. I found him one day near the edge of our wood line, standing just inside its border. We made friends quickly, as children do, eating wild strawberries and climbing high into trees, taking naps in a swale of sweetgrass. As the friendship grew, I tried to draw him home, but he would shake his head silently in refusal. One day we found a clutch of baby rabbits, disrupted by a neighborhood cat. One baby remained alive. I clutched it to my chest, ready to run home to get my mother's help. When I reached for my friend to pull him along, he read the intent in my eyes and pulled away. Dark and tousled, he backed up and I ran on. As months turned into years, it became apparent that he was afraid. Two years later, our parents told my sister and me of an impending move to Maine. For days I searched for my friend, knowing I could not affect their decision and desperate to see him. When I finally found him, he said he was bound to this place. He would never be allowed to leave it to visit me. Disbelieving the loss, I said hurtful things. We had to explore a new place together, and who would tell me stories of the real People? He didn't care, I told him. Day after day, I looked for him again to ask forgiveness, but he never reappeared.

Noting my sadness, mother bent to me. I mentioned my dark companion to her. For many months I had babbled on about adventures with this small companion. Now concern wrinkled my mom's brow; she told me the boy had never existed. "We never saw you with him," she said. "Only you alone." Because they were accustomed to my frequent conversations with myself, they had never thought to question me.

The new house in Maine was a huge, sprawling Main Street original. Only the third house built at the town's founding, it had been the home of the town's doctor and included a stable. The 200-year-old structure had a wraparound porch and a three-story barn. Despite this and an ornate, pillared façade with sweeping staircase, the price was very low. A bit suspicious about this, my parents were told that the house had been sold several times, but no buyers had stuck. My favorite place was the barn, which had housed the town's horses, feed, and tack. The barn's upper two stories were still sundrenched spaces full of interesting hiding places. One of these was a secret upstairs entrance into the body of the house. Antique furniture, discarded wooden toys, and Tiffany lampshades collected dust, which swirled in motes in the afternoon sun. There were hay windows front and back, and an old orchard fronting the woods behind. The house had come into possession of the town's physician, with a surgery added some years later. My first exploration of the cavernous tin-ceilinged rooms told me where I would choose to play.

The communal rooms held warm, safe feelings, while some of the private quarters and the surgery left me breathless with their cold, heavy malice. My room was closest to the stable, with a heavy door opening into the second floor of the barn. The room felt protected and warm if a bit wistful. There was almost an echo there, like the pause within a conversation between two people. But I ran without stopping up the sweeping staircase and past a smaller bedroom where the air hung in dark, thick clouds. The family's two large dogs would sometimes refuse to climb the stairs at night, growling and bristling at the bottom and refusing to go further. The path to my room, without lights, seemed long on those nights.

It can be amazing how young people adapt. Even the unusual can become a part of the customary landscape. As the days passed, there were friends to meet, chores to finish, and grades to manage. When the days were long, the woods became a place of retreat and solace. I was just able to see the darkened windows of the rear of the house from a sunlit portion of woods where I sat, clasping my knees, in a patch of red trillium.

The first of the obvious encounters with the house came with a gentle knocking on the barn side of my door. It would come at odd hours, a gentle but unexpected interruption of sleep. At first it seemed a part of dreams. Several days would pass and then the knock would awaken me again. Eventually it came while I was wide awake. It was the middle of the night. As realization came, my heart beat with trepidation. I resolved to find the cause. I crept to the door and bent forward in a protective crouch, sweat jumping out on my face and throat. The air was cold on the droplets on my skin. With flashlight in hand, I brought my face to within inches of the door, so close that my facial hair began to tickle in the air and stand up. I opened the door and snapped on the light in a single motion. The cold air hit me as the light reflected from a jumble of paper boxes and crates, but nothing except dust motes floated in the light. Backing into my room, I quietly closed the door.

These events continued, and soon the crying began. It was not a frightful sound, just a soft sorrow at the edge of my consciousness. There was no sign of aggression, and I found myself singing quietly to the voice's owner. When my voice was added, the crying would stop, and for that night there would be peace. At about the same time, my sister across the hall began to dream of a much more oppressive presence, one that would sweep her off her feet and propel her down the large central staircase. After several incidences of this and the dogs' refusal to mount the stairs, our parents began to ask questions. People in town all seemed to know about the house. They told a story about the town's doctor, who had been pushed down the stairs in a violent encounter with his wife. The man had died there at the bottom of the stairs. For years, the couple had been unhappy and slept apart, the doctor in my room and his wife in my sister's at the top of the stairs.

Life seemed a different world in the daylight. My father lost his job and found another which involved working at night, so I inherited a new set of chores. One was to let the two German shepherds out before the house closed down at night. With Main Street bustling out front, the dogs were released into the old orchard, lit at the far end of the field by a single streetlight. A picket fence bordered the property with its nearest neighbor. Caution was needed, as bear and deer had been seen in the old orchard. One night I ushered the dogs along the back of the barn, slowing their pace with my knees as they raced to the door, jumping with and over each other in their race to be out. As I opened the barn door, the dogs surged out and I saw a lone figure on the lawn. It was a young boy of perhaps eleven or twelve, and the dogs noticed him almost immediately. The boy pivoted and ran toward the abutting fence as I yelled for him to stop running. Never aggressive, the dogs chased the child, their barking accompanied by a strange, anxious baying. I, too, had begun to run, afraid that they would catch him. For the first time, I noticed the boy's strange vintage clothes: dark formal slacks and a white, bloused shirt and dress shoes. The boy's form rose, reaching the apex of the fence, bent to clear the top rung, faded…and disappeared. The dogs wheeled away in surprise, turning off at the last minute to avoid the fence. Their hair stood up along their shoulders and backs in frantic tufts.

Shortly after this incident, the fabric of the family began to fray. While each family member would later wonder why we did not share the many similar incidents that came to punctuate our lives, we each seemed to retreat into our own way of coping. While there was a cooperation for basic survival, our father began to withdraw into anger, and old war wounds seemed to rise again to the surface. My sister retreated into her own world, and there were problems at school. Worried about our financial survival, my mother began working long hours. None of us seemed to notice that outside the house our feelings were lighter and different.

My father's hunting companion for years, I couldn't wait to escape to the mountain hunting camp where the men told deer stories and my father seemed more at peace. I was a crack rifle shot; with a hat and heavy clothing, it was easy for the men to forget I was different from them. It didn't seem to matter. Only in camp did my dad still tell stories about the Old Times. I was treated as an equal there, and had earned my way into the others' respect by having an uncanny sense about the location of deer. It was a matter of some joking: "Would the witchy one like to project where the deer are today?" The older men would smile fondly as they ran cleaning cloths across the silky blackness of their rifle barrels. Each trip was a strategy session where I would pit my knowledge against the skill of wily old swamp bucks. Sharing in the tasks of killing and cleaning, I listened to the respectful words and occasional tears my father would shed for an animal so taken. "Thank you for giving your body to us," he would murmur.

Once home, the reality of daily life settled on Dad's shoulders again. He lost yet another job in an effort to pursue a long-hoped-for dream. As my parents tried to cope, I became absorbed in my dreams. I had begun to have several repetitive stories play out, each with astounding details of sight, smell, and sound. Family problems faded into the distance in an overly large house where the adults made the decisions. Life could be sweet alone in my sunlit room with its towering maple tree outside.

One dream was in a Civil War setting. I was a young slave owner's daughter walking a well-worn path across a rolling lawn into a distant rail yard. There I would examine and touch the train cars, tracing their painted letters. Years later, I re-walked the same scene in hypnosis, able to tell my waiting practitioner each of the letters and words and the colors of each car. Past torn-up track and rusting metal, I moved in what seemed like memory, with an antebellum house in the background. At the end of each walk, I came to a dip between hillsides, which had accumulated a pool of spring rainwater. In the pool lay a Union soldier, whose glazed blue eyes reflected only the sky. The dream would end as I met the eyes of a tall black man. Each time it happened, I would feel a shock of recognition and would know him as a trusted friend.

In another, I was a wealthy older woman in a large house in the 1940s. The house was on a river at the outskirts of New York City. The rooms were filled with expensive furnishings, flower arrangements, and place settings, which I would go on to describe in precise detail to my curious family for years. In this dream, the table was always set for friends and family long gone, the belongings the only consolation for a life lived alone. I would grieve for the loss of a son.

It was another, however, that would come to be the heart path to my future. I became aware that there were some dreams which had an entirely different feel and fabric: Instead of the random themes and known characters, some few had the feeling of memory. They contained a sense that they were separate from my teen self, as if belonging to an adult with its own emotions in situations separate from my own. The dream would begin in a clearing at the edge of a wood. A trail ran through the forest, becoming wider and with fewer trees and tangled undergrowth as I moved along. I was conscious of being present in the dream as usual. I carried a long wooden bow. In the dream, a shot rang out, and then another, and I began to run. My nerves were tight with concern, which increased as I approached a small village. The trail became multiple paths as I raced to a domelike shelter. Inside were skins and soft, piled greens, but the dwelling was otherwise unoccupied. Concern became alarm as I ran on, dropping quickly into several other dwellings before rounding to the right, headed for open ground. The trees continued to thin, allowing bands of light into the path and dappling the leaf cover in changing patterns. As a gust of wind blew a branch across the path, I raised my arm to push it aside and caught a glimpse of my own forearm. Reddish-brown skin thinly covered banded muscle, and the hand was that of a mature young male with supple, squared fingertips. Then the image was swept away as the trees gave way to an open field. Rounded thunderclouds wrestled with sparks of sunlight, bright in the sky. In the afterglow, it took "me" (the young man) a moment before my (his) eyes adjusted to the figures struggling before me. Brown, lithe figures fought hand to hand with several White men. Stepping back for a moment, he (I) scanned the field, looking for a woman who would be harboring a small boy of four. A most special boy. A remembered piece of me felt sad at previous conflict with his mother (my wife?), but feelings for the boy were uncomplicated. I did not see the child, but my eyes noted the boy's mother at the edge of the field. She was surrounded by a group of White men and horses. I called to two of the Native combatants, who acknowledged my presence on the field and regrouped to the left. As he (I) dove toward the woman at the rear of the field, the sun struck the rounded hill before me and backlit an opponent. Sun-struck for a moment, I smoothly swung a heavy club in my right hand to where a shoulder should be. A White man stepped across the fallen body of a fellow to meet the blow. As my dream self drove the club to batter the man's clavicle inward, there was a tremendous painless shock, and white light poured in from behind. A final afterimage registered in his (my) brain of a dark horse running behind defender and attacker, its mane and withers on fire. There was the image of a shocked female face, mouth open in a soundless scream. Then all was peace and warmth and rising.

I sat up in the bed in a pool of eastern light, early-morning sun dappling the white curtains and ruffling my mop of red-gold hair. It took a minute for my vision to clear, wind quickly cooling my sweat-soaked skin into goosebumps. Raising my arm, I checked to make sure it was my own pale skin. I knew that memory had caught up with me, draping itself like a warm skin across my shoulders. This dream had its own palpable weight and form. I remembered lying in my crib many years before and feeling as though my skin was too small to fit my intended purpose. Though I could not yet say what form the purpose would take, it had found me. I knew that I had only to wait for it to speak again. The first iteration of the dream had occurred just two weeks before I sat near a rain-soaked window in Maine, catching in my own reflection a somber and sober look others might have noted as alien. In that time, mirrors had become troublesome. For as I stood before the gilded glass, my blue eyes looked back; they appeared shielded and intro-spective. As the dream came and went, more feelings and memory came along; and I was never quite sure whose image might be looking back.

Katetin's Song

Katetin stood at the edge of the pond, its surface throwing ripples and wavelets. A woman emerged from the one-room schoolhouse at the top of the hill and strode toward the pool. Katetin could see her past the blue-flag iris lining the bank. The woman's form reflected from the water as if she had sprouted like another spring flower. The child closed her eyes and her throat closed up. She drew a deep breath and pushed Instip behind her in a protective gesture. Instip was different now, not wanting to leave her side. The woman dropped a blue plaid shawl from her hair to her rounded shoulders, shifting a basket of clothes beneath her arm. Katetin had seen children coming and going from the small structure, and the woman spoke to them kindly. Instip's eyes shifted between the woman and his sister's face. They had waited so long for Mother to return as she had promised. The hillside hadn't changed much as the years following the battle had passed, but neither had Katetin and Instip. The time drew long. Surely it could not hurt to look again into the woman's bright face. They had stood here many times now, hoping to see her turn and notice them.

Katetin had grown lonely. They still had the Wind Spirit and Its home in the great oak tree. The Spirit was kind; it had swept Katetin and Instip up as the furry White man had descended on the children, firelight backlighting him like the bear he appeared to be. As the man bent, his hands full of harm, the Shape Changer had come between them, wrapping the children in windswept arms and bearing them away. "First Children," It cried, "you must move on." But Katetin remembered her mother's words and reached for her brother's hand. "We must wait here," she said. "Mother told us to wait for her." And so the Guardian had nestled them at the base of Its tree. The morning after the battle, the meadow remained. But for days into years into numberless years, still their mother had not returned.

Today Katetin approached the woman in plaid again, coming so close as to stir the air between them. She placed all of herself, all her heart wishes and soul, into the breath she blew. With it she wished herself back into her mother's soft arms as she held out her own.

The older White woman turned away from the clothes she had laid out to dry. Her blue eyes crinkled as she raised her arm to shade her face. The wind blew a soft sigh to her. The sun's rays angled such that, for a moment, in its beams she could see a small figure with dark eyes and arms outstretched. She had felt the small presence before, but told herself it was an old woman's fancy. Still, she was a Scotswoman and a bit fey. So she bent over, hiking her long skirt a bit, and laid a gentle hand upon the memory of a child's cheek. The image had been only momentary and had long since faded.

And so it went for a number of years. Katetin would stop her play in the meadow and follow along behind the older woman, who would nod at her presence and march on. Sometimes the woman would finish her chores to find unexpected flowers on the back stoop. Sometimes she would pass an evening making grass toys or dolls. She would place them in a clear spot in the field and wait for them to be found. Occasionally her students would find them with the grass stems beaten down all around. If she sensed small eyes upon her as dusk approached and twilight settled over the hill, she would sing songs from a place across the great sea. Her father had taught her the Gaelic, so she sang to the children the songs of the sea, of the wind and its perennial loneliness. And the children knew that she understood.

People said it was sad when she passed alone, long after her students had grown and gone. But two remained with her that night as the candlelight flickered out. They placed upon her body a doll made of grass and a Wind Spirit guided the Scotswoman home.

Linda's Song

And so it seems time to step through a door and into the story in a different way. For I am not the child I was in those days, my body grown from youth to motherhood and from mother into elder. Through my teen years, the dream of being a Native hunter came and went, always filling me with a sense of strength and purpose. Odd commonalities in the memory-laden dreams became evident.

There was always a single person whom I encountered in different forms in each dream. Feelings came, and the knowledge that the small boy in the Native village I had searched for was a son. An aching loss and need to find him brought confusion for an adolescent not yet out of her teens when the dream first began. There was no clear-cut vision of where this all might go; only a sense that I had another chance at a purpose interrupted, a task waiting to be revealed.

Family life became harder. Our father's search for work took him far out of state for longer periods, often in the depth of winter. I took on many of his chores as Mother worked. When he did return, time had stopped for him. He found neither the pliant child nor the adoring companion of earlier years, but another adult with her own ideas. I found it easier to do the same things I'd become accustomed to as his presence came and went. After two years mostly alone and preparing for college, I kept a tight schedule of school, chores, athletics, and homework. There was no time left for the ups and downs of his successes and failures, though I wished him well. I was not disrespectful. I just continued the drive forward. My parents began to argue at night, and more and more frequently it was about me. My pull away saddened him, and it became impossible to please him. No grade, performance, or artwork was adequate. Finally he began to climb the stairs to get me from bed, exhausted and half asleep, to account for some small failing. As my seventeenth year passed, there was a night when the battle raged into early morning hours and ended with him striking me. I failed an important test that day, and I knew things had to change. I knew he lived with the daily struggle of a war that never ended, and at the base of his own anger was the fear that I would fail in the same ways. There was no worry of that: I was sure success was coming beyond the front door of a house where too many unhappy memories lived. As our family struggles grew, the energy in the house seemed to gather into an oppressive force of its own, tamping both the creativity he needed and my will to change it.

That fight cost me the top of my class but little more. Within a month, the race to graduation meant finishing tasks and keeping on track. Classmates planned parties on the lakes, got married, or separated to go on to college. On a rainy Saturday in April, as a final loomed on Monday, I had lain down to rest in the early afternoon. I remember the rain running down the glass in silver streaks as a mist drifted through the back orchard. The mountaintop behind it rose like the silhouette of a horse's back until a cloud sank and obscured it. My eyes grew heavy with the sight of it. The screen door to the backyard slammed and my mother's voice rose into the room below mine as she called to my father. She had asked for the money to buy material for a prom dress the week before and received no answer. I heard her raise the issue again, carefully couching her request. Their voices rose and fell, an even exchange which became shorter and more clipped. I heard reason change to concern. "She's already like an old woman," my mother said. "Too many chores and not enough joy. Where is the harm?" she asked, and then, "Her life isn't over, even if you feel yours is."

I heard him rise from his chair and his steps became rapid as he headed for the stairs. I stood up from my bed as my hand closed around the base of a heavy goose-necked lamp. I shifted it upward as the sound of a slap ricocheted downstairs. I heard my father's voice rise with the force of absolute soul-wrenching anguish. "I'll never let it happen to her. It'll end here first," he roared, and his feet hit the stairs.

I swear today that all of my hairs rose in a smooth wave from my head to my feet as I began to move toward the stairs. Afraid to run toward danger but unwilling to be trapped in a closed space, I kept moving forward, the lamp cocked at my hip. For the first few steps, I felt nothing but the desperate urge to survive, then a sudden uncertainty. Was this how every child felt as childhood dropped away? Then a sense of peace and power welled up, bearing me on and upward as if subsumed by a force much larger than myself. I felt an older presence wrap around me as I met my father at the top of the stairs. It was as if the force of three lifetimes and as many relationships rose up to protect me in a visceral surge of muscle memory. Bringing the lamp up in a smooth arc, I said, "Stop. Never again will you strike me. If you do, I'll kill you. Stop!" He stopped three steps below me and his face cleared and closed. Present inside his body once more, he turned and made his way downstairs.*

It was the last time I remember feeling alone with fear. The sensation of being protected and enclosed traveled with me as I ended my time at home. My mother arranged for me to spend the summer away with a beloved aunt, and college waited in the fall. For a brief time, there was just play, rest, and sun. When I glanced in a mirror apprehensively, I expected to see the result of my ragged last decade, but it did not show there. Youth called from a white sand beach, the drone of cicadas drowning out echoes from a cold Maine spring. And for a time I answered.

When fall came, I returned to attend the University of Maine, penniless but sure my grades would earn me a place. The next two years were spent in a competitive school program where I taught to help pay my tuition. As sophomore year came to an end, I found a darker edge to the competition. It appeared that academic survival could be bought or lost in the

* On the recording referred to in the introduction, the Guardian's voice said that he says "Stop!" when my voice is not being heard, that his "Stop!" is bigger than my "Stop."

dark of an after-hour's consult. "Not until hell freezes over" would I barter myself for a bell curve, I told a person of power. And though the Guardian presence stirred again, it was unnecessary. Fear had departed years before and I had hit my stride. I did the work and learned the limits of those who would use power badly. Though I paced just outside its reach, the days passed and I was protected by strength from the inside. "All of a piece," I heard my mother's voice repeat.

It was at the end of that year that I was reassigned to work on campus teaching transitional English to Native American youth accepted for the fall. As part of this, I was assigned as a liaison between the University and Native mentors on campus led by an older Native man. He was an imposing figure with a great expanse of chest and shoulder, and large expressive hands. He wore a turquoise ring on one finger of an enormous hand. His voice first heard was a soft, echo-y rumble. He must have been in late middle age then, hair just going to gray. What first impressed me as fearsome was soon to be shown to be an intense focus on whomever he spoke with. There were spaces between his words unlike those of anyone I'd ever known, each thought followed by a pause as he watched his words and gestures be received.

It was the era of the Maine Indian Land Claims Settlement. Although the session had been called to discuss the role of the University in the future of Native children, it did not take long for the subject to expand to the troubled history between Maine's First People and the Newcomers. As my own family's longtime arbitrator, I found the discussion fascinating, totally forgetting the color of my own skin among the Penobscot group's members. As they talked about the benefits and deficits of the Agreement and their possible consequences, their voices rose. Initially buried in my own concerns about the students arriving, I missed the fact that things had become heated.

When a tense silence followed, I felt a prickling uneasiness and awareness that I had become the focus of attention. I looked up, unsettled and unsure where the discussion had ended. Without as much as a word, my Native mentor's large, dark hand settled over mine, engulfing its pale shape with his own. I was reminded of a great bear, the hand at once powerful and gentle in its motion. He never looked at me, his voice instead calming the others in the room. It was as if there was a collective release. The gesture was at once inclusive and protective but not condescending and placed no fault on the others around him. I was reminded of my own gentle guardian, and I would review the memory of his subtlety and kindness to a strange White girl many times in the future. In a way, it helped me decide a piece of who I would become. I had known my part in the meeting would be a listening one, but I had not expected to be derailed by my own inattention into an awareness of discord both sudden and intense. For a few brief moments, my thoughts had slipped so smoothly between the Native person I had been 400 years ago and the role I had now that I had failed to register my current skin color as different from theirs. It made me realize I needed to take something more than just English back into the classroom.

When I really tuned in to the words the Native people spoke and watched the gestures of that powerful, bearlike man, I understood the importance of the future successes of these children. Over time, I became accustomed to the nuances of their feelings: The cadence of speech allowed for quiet meanings between the words, flowing among them. It awoke something familiar in me as well, as if awakening from a long sleep. I wove the same rhythm into my interactions with their children. I heard their anger under taut control, drew it into the assignments I gave, and taught them how to make the English words carry power. Anger from suppressed emotion could be expressed with determination and precision. Most of all, I wanted them not to lose themselves into what we were. There were challenges to my authority, my skin color, and my gender that summer. Sometimes these were funneled into assignments, other times into discussion. Somehow we found a type of balance, I think, where basic trust could live and grudging respect could grow.

When I left school, I left with the man I would marry and who would father my children. He was a gentle man from an old French family. I would watch him from across a distance, picking him out easily from among the others. The others would hunch, minds on the cold or their next class, minds far away. My man would come into sight on a straight, grounded path, graceful and present in his own body. Years later I would watch footage of a male moose walking through fallen trees and rocky scree and smile at the similarity. He was quiet in temperament, seeming reserved and older than his years in some ways while innocent in others. As we entered the adult world, he would walk into a work experience expecting to be listened to and respected. Many times he would be disappointed and turn inward, becoming restless with others' expectations. Always his words were measured and sparse, the emotion buried deep inside. My careful mother was guarded about that tendency, but my father embraced him as a companion and son, finding an unaccustomed connection with a young man already tested by life. Life was not easy in northern Maine.

As the years passed, we became a young family. Our son joined us first; he was a child with an open, liquid personality who radiated peace and acceptance. We called him "liquid sunshine" and he filled us with his joy in life. Our daughter came four years later and was as outgoing and inquisitive as our son was accepting. Bold and fearless, she struggled from containment of any sort. Though very different, we sensed they might complement each other's needs as they grew until someday we were gone.

Once the children were no longer helpless, my thoughts turned to how we might guide them in Spirit. After searching my inner and outer landscapes for meaning, my husband and I agreed to raise them in the context of shamanic journeying, always hoping they might find their own answers in life. There were snippets of memory for me of a rigorous training and the rewards of spiritual contact, and a trustworthy group existed in our area. Each of my family's souls filled me with joy, and I fell in love with them all, watching them grow by the day. For a while, the magic held.

Too soon for all of us, I began to notice my husband's struggle to fit into the nine-to-five world. With the pressure of a growing family, he tried harder to fit into a cookie-cutter corporate environment. He believed he could bring creativity and compassion into an increasingly technological setting, and at first there were successes, but the pace and need for constant growth in industry soon washed over him like a wave. To him, if a job could be done well in a few hours, it was enough for one day. He simply did not understand the need to be bound to a schedule. I recognized the familiar pattern of my own childhood in the man I married, but he was not like my father, and anxiety and the collapse of confidence drove him inward. There was no chasing him inside; our joy seemed to make his unhappiness worse. Restless and frustrated, he finally left us.

As our marriage had started to teeter, his father died. In the days immediately following this, his much younger mother came forward with an unexpected statement. After the gathering of family, she announced that her family was *not* just Canadian French, but Native American as well. She had been precluded through the length of her marriage from discussing this, and had not been allowed to tell her children. I watched my husband's reaction to this news as he moved from shock to realization. His face crumpling in tears, he raised both hands to cover his face. I will never know exactly what this revelation meant to him, or what made it all become clear that he would never fit well into the expected mode of business. I do remember it seemed to solidify his decision to leave, but it had nothing to do with shame. On one of our last days together, he asked me to find out as much as I could about his "other" family and to keep our children close to it as much as possible.

And because I loved him, I did. He left us then, to find a place where he could roam the woods in solace. Big woods, where he could learn his own heart without costing his children the pain he felt himself. Freed by our interest, his mother began to tell old stories from Canada and northern Maine, and though our family got smaller, we went on.

The children grew, and my husband kept his promise to remain in their lives. We worked hard to adjust to our roles apart but raised the children together as much as possible. We practiced hard on humor and kindness. Eventually I remarried to a wonderful man who treasured the chance to be a father to my children. Henry joined our family. We trained together in martial arts and became Reiki practitioners. As part of a community of martial artists, we shared child rearing and teaching in the larger community. After 20 years we opened our own school on the bank of the Kennebec River. And that's when things began to change again.

It was in my fiftieth year that we moved our small martial arts school to the Cliffside on the Kennebec River. The meadow was sunny and cold on that day in early spring, the snow barely melting into the icy pools of the intervale. The sky was tumultuous, with powerful dark cumulus clouds backlit in white by the warming sun. Flat splats of rain dropped in patches on the meadow, and were lit up by a large silver maple by a small, round pond. Nearly buried in brush was what looked like an old foundation, its rocky base flanked by an old patch of daffodils. Their expectant faces gave a settled-looking, homey wave to me as the wind moved among them. I searched the meadow for other hints of its nature and found it in grassy tussocks and emerging wildflowers. Ripples echoed themselves in geometric patterns across the pools of spring melt. A Wind Spirit lived here, I was sure of it. As I turned my face to the clouds above, the sun broke through and my face was struck by flat plops of rain. Yes, this could be home.

Rarefaction

Katetin's father turned his broad face to the sky as the cloud cover began to break. It appeared that the speaker across the river would have sun to warm him today in his speech to the gathered people. His mind traveled back a year, replaying a conversation with a cousin from up north. This man had traveled with a group of bandsmen to Kebik to request the presence of one of the Blackrobes. This was so that the people could understand the nature and character of the White man's God. It was said that protection might come to those on the southern river, trapped between the English to the south and east and the deep-woods tribes of the north and west. Some said that the rituals of the gentler Blackrobes were not dissimilar to their own. There, some had found structure and peace as opposed to the harshness of the English God. One Native man, Mejachkawit, had been instructed by the French Church in Kebik. It was he who was supposed to appear today, first within the walls of the trading post and then to any Native families farther upriver. While he did not subscribe to White man's ways, Katetin's father knew traditional life was changing under the pressure of contact. He had only to remember the incident which happened to his family the day before to see its effects: that when people did not understand each other's deeper beliefs, conflict could arise with startling suddenness. He was of a mind to listen to Mejach-kawit's words from the western bank with his family close by. Only then would he travel south to retrieve the fortune in furs they had lost. In the meantime, the family would remain safe on the high western shore.

As if such thoughts summoned his own, Mejachkawit turned his body north, where the river bend appeared just within sight. He had a small group to accompany him, two Native guides from the area and a young Native apprentice bound to return to the Priory in Kebik.

Mejachkawit was a thoughtful man, a lover of the beauty of words. He found meaning in the symmetry of ritual, thought, and word. He had been touched by the Blackrobes' concern for the Native people, especially when it came to the White man's use of alcohol as a bargaining item. He had seen firsthand the devastation of spirit that arose from the pressure on his People, their search for safety in a world now filled with starvation and illness. He loved the stories of the Christ's gentleness with children and the use of ritual to calm the spirit. There was discipline in the teachings which said that deprivation of the will led to strength in spirit. The Blackrobes had been interested in the language and culture, inasmuch as they could understand it. When he had spoken just hours before to the British settlers at the post, he had expected common ground. Did not the English and French purport to believe in the same God? He had thought that the commonality of belief could do much to stabilize the tension of life on the knife edge. He hoped to unite what beliefs the two cultures shared with his own, rather than focus on what divided them. Instead he had encountered censure and a terse rendering of the differences in Christian beliefs. It was as if the post's advisors and followers were speaking of a different God, one with many more rules. And there was no way to be prepared for the vehement rhetoric of the English people, who had themselves once been a tribal people at war over religious doctrine. A war which had lasted for over a hundred years and brought its people to Native shores fleeing its persecution. * Perhaps their gods were different after all, but he would speak a language of inclusion.

And so Mejachkawit's footsteps fell more heavily as he turned his head north, where he would speak to members of his own People. He had hoped to tell them there could be a meeting of hearts they could share with the newcomers at the post. The Fathers in Kebik had spoken with him about a chapel on the river where all could be welcome. Faced

---

* The Hundred Years War, fought by England and France from 1337–1453. This war caused a grievous taxation of their peasant populations, causing uprisings in the midst of the Black Death. This, in turn, also saw an enormous rift in the Catholic Church. European religious conflict was brought to these shores and in turn affected those who were Indigenous here.

with the difference in interpretation, the tension of the settlers had flared into anger and Mejachkawit had been asked to leave. An escort saw his party out, and with a heavier heart he complied.

There were other eyes and ears at the post that day. After traveling downstream to try to unload the stolen furs, the party of young outsiders discovered that word of the theft had preceded them. The mood of the traders at Richmond was not good. With food and money running low, the youths had decided to turn northward again. They would need to take an inland route past the encampment on the Kennebec's western bank. They were not aware of the camp's size or numbers and were both frustrated and concerned about encountering the Native family again. It was at that point that they passed the crowd attending Mejachkawit's speech and listened to the tension erupt among the participants. Perhaps there were seeds to sow here, a distraction which might serve to boil the tensions in a useful direction and further enrich the rogue merchants. For there was surely no lack of fodder to fuel the flame of fear between the two peoples. That much was certain.

And so the young merchant found himself in the smoky entrance of the Meetinghouse at Cushnoc by the noon hour. He picked the remnants of his sparse midday meal from his teeth in desultory fashion as he waited for the settlement's councilman to see him.

Once admitted, he told a story to provoke a specific reaction, describing the sight of the Natives' council fire three nights previous. With his words, the People's dances of thanks for winter's bounty became twisted into lustful gestures and debauchery, their chants of gratitude becoming an exhortation of unseen and unknown demons and spirits. He was certain their enthusiasm was attributable to alcohol procured at the post.

The councilman was a busy man, but he was a fair one. The pace of development in the settlement sometimes threatened to overrun time and materials so far north on the river. It had been a dry spring, and tides were low on the river. Lumber was in high demand and ships were struggling to dock with needed tools and supplies. He made the argument that the Native people had long been engaged in the practice of dance, and reminded the young merchant that dance alone was not a sin, only the intention to produce lust in others. And if the Native men engaged in alcohol, it was certainly a vice introduced by unethical practice among Whites.

The young trader thought quickly. He had to find a lever in the stresses the fledgling post was facing to divert the area's attention from their progress north. What might cause enough division in the rhythm of the days to allow them to resume travel north unseen? He reminded his elder that even when the intent of sin remained unspoken, it must be aggressively dealt with to prevent its bloom. And he created a story whereby Katetin's father and uncle had been observed just the day before following one of the settler's wives from the post. Their eyes, he stated, had not been either innocent or untutored. He reminded the older man that only today had the Native Jesuit been driven from the post, and that the tribes had been under tutelage of the French for some time. They could no longer be accorded ignorance of Christian belief. And still, he stated, they practiced heathen and lustful dancing. It was only a matter of time before the smoke became a flame and someone's wife or child might be injured. After all, wasn't the Native speaker appearing before them as they spoke? Who could say what might happen tomorrow if their dancing tonight was repeated and the Jesuit incited their anger?

The administrator's eyebrows lowered into a single dark line. There was something in the trader's story that seemed to require more thought. But the younger man had been present at the post on two occasions and had wrapped his story around both religious doctrine and the differences in faith as described by others at the post. The older man was needed elsewhere; he assured the young trader he would speak to the others in council assiduously and discuss what might be done.

At about the same time, Katetin's father had positioned himself apart from the rest of the band. His position halfway down the western river-bank allowed him an unobstructed view of the eastern shore and its southern approach. Two canoes had been pulled ashore after a several-mile journey from Taconic upriver. The river burbled and broke around their beached prows. He saw the younger Mejachkawit arrive, attended by his guides and apprentice. The guides had set up in a cleared area at the river's edge where there was ample room for sitting. Katetin's father dropped his weight silently, shifting onto his heels and steadying himself with one extended finger on a nearby stone. It had taken some time for the people to gather, but it appeared the speaker would soon begin. There was a palpable air of excitement. Mejachkawit's eyes met those of the older clan leader on the hill above and acknowledgment was made. Katetin's father read peace and certainty in the younger man's face. With a nod, he stood and turned about, climbing the gentle slope beside a small waterfall and positioning himself again within the wood line. He glanced northward and noted the distance from the meeting place to the campsite of his people, and crouched down to wait.

Katetin listened to the soft murmur of her parents' speech as her father ducked back inside their shelter to retrieve his bow. She passed a hand across her forehead as she tried again to wrestle her small adversary into a fresh clout. A shower of cattail fluff, milkweed down, and carefully dried moss erupted from the bundle. As she scooped to gather it up, the baby flipped completely, seeming to sprout extra arms and legs. One of them found her belly as she stood again, finally plunging skin, fluff, and baby into the same space. She placed a slender hand on his rounded belly and half turned to listen to Father's instruction. Having listened to much of Mejachkawit's speech, he was leaving for Cushnoc. He advised her mother that all seemed calm on the west bank, but she was to leave the children in camp high on the hill with the elders. Several of the women kept watch at the tree line and could listen to the speaker but go no further. Some of the townspeople had made the walk upriver to hear Mejachkawit, which meant that the post would be quieter. Perhaps someone there would have noticed the young merchant's departure with the family's furs.

Her father bent slowly to touch Katetin's cheek. Perhaps that little drum might find its way back to camp. She was such a good child, quiet and brave. Then he rose, placed a hand on his wife's shoulder, and stepped outside. Her mother watched him stride away and turned to Katetin. "Stay with your brothers," she said.

Four young merchants accompanied the wagon as it left Cushnoc. The old trail followed the Kennebis, meandering around landforms to some extent but mostly keeping the river in sight. This was especially true where high ridges overlooked deer trails or river access points. Because of the view to the south, the young men knew the trail would pass close to the Natives' campsite. This would be true until they reached Taconic before swinging gradually northwest. Once scarcely more than a footpath, it had stretched to the width of a wagon as trade had increased between Narantsouak and Cushnoc some thirty miles south.

The trader men grew quieter as they scanned the wooded trail ahead. About a hundred yards farther on, the trail was lit by a plume of sunlight. The young merchant was able to pick out the patterns of scrub oak and alder which marked the widening of the trail and the meadows where the trees thinned into the Native campsite. Ridges rose to the right, abutting the hundred-foot drop to the river. The entire area had been a glacial scour thousands of years before, the ice masses pushing rock and detritus over the cliff. Long ago covered by thin topsoil and wildflowers, the soil was perfect for sun-loving berries and scarlet lilies. The group watched the clearing carefully as they approached. At one point, they heard the rise of voices on the wind, reflected back by the water and hollow hillside. Then a ridge deadened the sound as they moved ahead with more stealth. The young Native priest had made clear the meeting's location, and raised voices this far upriver made it plain. Hoping still to find common ground, Mejachkawit had invited the town's inhabitants to come and listen again.

Katetin's father removed the bow from its slung position over his shoulder and carried it low as he approached the trail. As he paused to listen, his brother also halted. Rising from the meadow's edge to their left, a mature red-tailed hawk rose from its mantled position over a kill and swept in front of the two men. Its flight was a graceful arc through the trees as it passed over the sandy trail, the streamers of sun lighting its feathers to gold. The men on the wagon turned to watch it go.

And then two things happened quite quickly. As the hawk's outline sailed in front of them, the wheel of the merchants' wagon dropped into a deep hole filled with spring melt unnoticed by the startled men. With a sharp crack, the spoke gave way and the vehicle listed. Katetin's father stepped noiselessly to the dark horse's bridle.

Mejachkawit drew a deep breath, pulling the essence of pine and soil from the ground through his feet and into his lungs in a smooth breath. His eyes were focused on a line of firs, and his spirit soared with the gentle message still echoing from the cliff face. He had checked the faces in front of him partway through his recital, and noted that there were more people gathered before him. He had lowered his tone, putting all his hopes for reconciliation into the melody of his words. Now, there was quite a group of settlers at the rear of the clearing. All were quiet now, the White settlers' reserve shuttering their faces and rendering them unreadable in the stillness that followed.

At that moment, a crack echoed from the opposite bank with the ricochet snap of a musket, and the crowd began to scatter. Echoes rippled outward from the walls of the cliff, then seemed to move inward to rumble again along the riverbed in long slow waves. In vain, the settlers peered up the wooded slope. But whatever had happened was hidden beyond the trees. Several men broke through the crowd to wade the shallow expanse of the river and began to scale the rocks beyond. Far above them at the meadow's edge, several of the Native men ran for the trail, while others became visible at the top of the cliff. They faced the White men rising along the cliff's rounded face.

As the echoes of the sharp report faded, Katetin's mother had begun to run. She stopped at the height of land to see her husband locked hand to hand with one of the young traders over the contents of a wagon, listed over to its right side. The dark horse at the wagon's front was desperately trying to pull its burden out of the trench, spittle lining its maroon lips, teeth bared and eyes rolling.

She wheeled about midway, turning abruptly toward the campsite at the sound of splintering wood and shot coming from the tree line. Shouts now echoed just out of sight over the bank as figures merged and struggled, looking for all the world like a worm trapped by a nest of ants. Smoke rolled up to meet a cloud of river fog as it slithered in a ghostly glide between the combatants. Katetin's mother could see her oldest child running from her position in the meadow toward a large oak downslope. As she opened her mouth to scream, her vision was filled by a tall stranger, hair wild and flying and far too close for her to stop. Love filled her last sight as she saw the daughter of her heart stoop to grasp something hidden at the tree's base. Then darkness came, and release.

The Guardian, the Shapechanger, rolled over onto its side, its winds becoming denser as it bent to catch the essence of the child Katetin. Old fall leaves stood on end and whirled about in pursuit as it dusted the stony hillside. The child's spirit hesitated, pulling itself back toward its physical body. A thought said, "Instip?"

And as the thought occurred, the child also rolled, her head coming gently to rest on the face of a wet, cool stone. A single drop of blood came to rest there. Then the energy within the child surged upward, entwining itself within the feathery plumes of the Guardian's embrace.

Katetin stood at the base of the guardian tree, her eyes trained on her father's tall figure. Instip sat facing the river, where he had remained motionless for three long days following the battle. Whatever was happening inside his small frame belonged to him alone. She had seen her father return to the hillside before dawn. Of her mother there had been no sign. He had begun to search the ground, kneeling now and again in the long grass and once had dropped his head into his hands in silent anguish. Although the fires had burned out, the very air had a charred, electrified feel as if a storm had just passed. Time itself seemed to be poised in balance, a wave at its peak before breaking. All the hairs on his arms had raised as if Spirit had passed close by. The clan chief had found the remains of the hide shelter, its contents scattered and muddied by spring rain and tracks. In his hand was a large stone axe head Katetin had seen him use for girdling young trees. He began to dig. As the sun broke over the eastern ridge, its rays fell in a broad semicircle and shone on the three cylindrical holes he had dug. She saw him rise and disappear into the mist and refracted sunlight, carrying a wrapped bundle which he lowered into the first of the holes. Then the wave broke: Time shifted sideways for Katetin and, for a period of time, she knew no more.

The incident at the river's edge sparked a meeting of concerned settlers. The discussion devolved quickly into polarized arguments when it was discovered that trouble had been brought amongst them by those outside the community. How quickly tempers had flared, precipitated by those with no investment in the outcome. Nerves were frayed. Some said it didn't matter who had started it; that remuneration had been made for the land occupied and now it must be held. Others felt helpless, having given everything they owned in exchange for passage to the

"New World." Most regretted and remembered stories from relatives in the Old Country. Those stories had told of wars which had displaced one group by another for over a thousand years. A heavy quiet weighed upon their souls. Something vital had changed for everyone since the attack. When the talking was done, a small group of men had agreed to accompany their womenfolk to the meadow on the hillside. There they placed three wooden crosses on brush-covered mounds. And if the silence echoed without a single birdsong, their hearts were too heavy to notice. Fearing a reprisal that would never come, they left the scattered detritus of the camp for the Wind to reclaim. In years to come, people on the trail came to know the place in their bones, for the Land cried its grief in a great echo of silence like the hollow heart of a drum.

The moments of the day can pass in typical fashion like a well-oiled machine, with only the slightest change of beat. But experiences which happen outside the ordinary can occur on the turn of a dime. The human animal will notice it, but then its busy brain restores a sense of order and the sensation passes. The truth of an odd happening exists within a pregnant pause: like not quite seeing something from the corner of your eye. At that moment, what is normal becomes worrisome, an awareness that the mind and eyes are being deceived. The sun continues to shine brightly, but the air becomes shadowed and chill. In that moment, possibility blossoms; the brain struggles for explanation and, finding none, moves on to another day in the ordinary. So it was on the day Katetin found me and mystery erased the ordinary for me like rain on dust.

Connection

AE

August of 2010 was a very warm season. I stood at the edge of the meadow, watching a harrier hawk hang in the air as I unwrapped a sweat-dampened tartan sash from my shoulder. We had returned home from the Maine Highland Games and were tired from the day and the crowds. As always, the drums and shrill pipes of the Games had brought the colors of my surroundings into sharp focus. As I traveled the road to the meadow site, my senses were engaged and the light seemed overly bright. High clouds piled up behind the western hills and cicadas buzzed. Bees were a slow drone in counterpoint among shafts of goldenrod and purple aster. The place hung still, no breath of wind among purple and yellow sunbursts, their heads hanging under the weight of the insects. Chipmunk stood frozen on the rail of the yurt. There was a sensation that time might have stopped as I walked slowly down the path. Turning to face the woods at Cliffside, my chest felt heavy. My heart rolled and it became hard to breathe. Just as I was becoming alarmed, the white outline of a child burst into my mind's eye, and a small voice said, "Find me!" The image was so intent with need that I rocked back on my heels, goosebumps chasing themselves in waves down my arms. "Find me," she sighed again. Then the Reiki in my hands lit up, and my vision cleared, pins and needles running from fingertips to elbows.

I stood still for several minutes afterwards, letting my impressions settle. My eyes were drawn to the right and down the path, where a large honeysuckle bush draped scarlet berries over the path. I lifted my palms to show their emptiness, walking slowly toward the bush and noticing the ebb and flow of energy to my hands. As the sensation became intense, I peeked around the bush. For an instant the vision flickered again. "Find me," she implored with a whisper and then was gone.

I kept the child at the edge of my consciousness for several days, thinking of her at the edge of sleep and weighing the sensation of her in my mind. I visited the spot occasionally, Reiki energy finding her signature, but she did not approach again. What had called to her initially? What had made her trust what she had seen? Then the memory of the day of the Highland Games returned.

Reaching into a wooden drawer, I found the now carefully folded sash and slung it over my shoulder. On arriving at the hillside, I draped the plaid over my right shoulder and made a bow on my left hip. "Where are you?" I called gently, but only the wind sighed in return. Finally I turned my back to the trail, calling my Reiki and placing my open hands behind my back. I rested them at my hips, palms upward behind me. "Come, dear one," I whispered, and waited. First one hand lit up, then the other. And a small hand laid itself gently on my upturned palm. At the moment of contact, I saw her again in my mind's eye. A small dark girl, all eyes and tied-back hair, stared back. She appeared to be eight or nine years old, a tenuous smile forming at the edges of her mouth. She turned then and brought forth a small boy of four or five. After a moment's hesitation, my right hand flared as he set his small palm upon it. Without words, they followed me along, me in front and them behind, until the signatures faded and all was still.

This became a habit as I made my rounds, weeding the restored areas, planting and mowing. I became adept at sensing them as they fell in behind me. At first I sang only small songs, always afraid to frighten them. The tone of our encounters was curious, a blend of joy and need when they realized I saw them. There were places in the open field where they loved to play and others which they seemed to avoid. After several encounters, the older child again seemed fearful. "Find me," she would say again. I thought about what it was I was supposed to find, and my urgency grew along with hers. I knew where the Reiki signatures were the strongest, but not how this was relevant. "Help me find where you are," I whispered. It struck me then what I hadn't seen: that whatever remained of them physically might still be here, under the grasses and flowers of the meadow. On that hunch, I mounted the riding lawn mower, determined to cover as much ground as possible while moving slowly enough to look for signs of disturbance. After a long period, my efforts were still unrewarded. To make matters worse, the heavy silver bangle I wore on my wrist had disappeared somewhere in the brush and grass. Irritation provided the impetus for me to call it a day.

Distracted from my original intent, the search for the circular bangle took the better part of two days. It had been a gift from my husband, and I couldn't believe the loss. I carefully searched every inch of the trails I'd covered, particularly those where I had encountered the children. On short mown grass, the search should have been annoying but brief. I repeated my efforts, surprised at the bangle's total disappearance.

To give me another focus, Henry showed me an aerial view of the river property taken several years previously. We had been using the geology of the site to plan and locate plant species in their optimum environments. As I picked up the images, I could feel the hair rise on my neck, for on the map there appeared three roughly cylindrical distortions of the land's surface just east of the height of land. They were obvious disturbances to the sand and gravel beneath the surface, the narrow cylinders in a line running roughly north to south in a semicircle. Knowing the layout of the area, all I could picture was that tall honeysuckle bush, behind which had crouched the image of a small Indian child.

I stood at the edge of the path the next morning and checked the area again, then stilled my mind. Spreading both hands palm up, I again wondered how the path could have swallowed such a substantial piece of jewelry. A random idea crossed my mind which logic tried at once to erase. "Dear child," I told her, "if you know where the bracelet is, place it where you are, and you can know that I will find you."

Early the next morning, I mounted the grumbling, belching old mower again and rode out. A part of me was sure the bangle's disappearance was permanent and felt this was most logical. An increasingly larger part of me, though, hoped for an interaction with Spirit, an opportunity to have an experience different from the ordinary. I swung around a corner where groundnut tendrils reached tentative fingers toward the path and into the shade of an area of whispering aspen; milkweed reached into a ragged patch of sunshine with their oval arms straining skyward. Just beyond their upraised arms dwelt the overgrown honeysuckle.

And at its base, a shining circlet of silver gleamed in the center of the path.

For several moments I could only stare. Carefully dismounting the mower, I approached the bangle, certain I would blink and have it be gone. Overcome with emotion, I knelt and placed my palms squarely on the warm earth. "I've found you. I'm here, little one," I murmured softly. A gentle sigh blew by on the wind. For a moment, time seemed to pull itself into slow motion, like a piece of machinery long unused; and then birdsong erupted from the trees in a cacophony of sound.

Something had changed for Katetin. She and Instip raced down the field, chasing the grumble of the woman's conveyance, stabbing the silver circlet with the pin she had fashioned for her game of ring-pin. With a deft flip of the wrist she lifted and flipped it until it lay in just the right spot at the head of the first of three mounds. She watched the woman rise and step to the next mound, and finally a third. Keeping them all in sight, the woman had bowed in respect and promised to visit often.

Something loosened and expanded for the child. She turned to find Instip smiling as well, his eyes bright and lit from within.

Summer passed quickly and the nights grew cool. We knew that soon winter would come and wondered where the children played when the snow and the wind turned the bounty of spring into a frigid, barren tundra. We wondered how to deepen the tie with the two and how we could communicate our support. We decided on a fire ceremony for a cool September night. By this time, we had sensed two other presences on the Land, one which the children seemed to try to avoid. It felt like a worry on the Land, a dark chaotic spot in the fabric of an otherwise well-knit tapestry. If not frankly disturbing, it did seem to constrict the youngsters' movement and hold them to itself. If we were to be gone while the Land slept, we wanted to be sure the children would be well. As Henry built a fire in the large fire pit, I walked to the honeysuckle and held out my hands. Almost immediately I felt their small presences, hands quickly dropping into my own. We walked the path to the fire pit, and I could sense their excitement and understanding. Could they remember such nights with their own family?

As we turned toward the fire, I could hear a loud, agitated rattle begin near the wood's edge and feel the children move behind me. Our dog's hackles rose, and she circled to the edge of the firelight. "Probably just a raccoon," Henry said softly. Sitting close to the fire, I began to sing an old Mi'kmaw song I had learned to sing to my own children. Sensing their fear, I pulled the energy of the children into my lap and encircled them. For nearly a half hour the creature moved around us in a circle, just beyond the light of the fire. The dog ranged to the limits we would allow her, lips pulled back over her teeth and growling low in her chest. It seemed very strange that a natural creature would move toward us in its distress with the entirety of the field available to escape contact.

Finally, it was as if the creature sensed that the children were protected in our care, and it slowly moved off, complaining in a ratchety tone as it faded into the distance. From that time forward, the air seemed lighter somehow, and the children less burdened. I mentioned the incident to an Indigenous acquaintance several months later. She told me a story of the "Little People." These were Nature Spirits who were sensitive to the presence of strangers and who could have either protective or mischievous reactions when their area was disturbed.*

When spring came, we couldn't wait to be back on the land. I hadn't stopped working all that long fall and winter, and had been in touch with a local researcher to learn more about the area's history. He had referred me to a well-known set of papers by Jesuit priest Father Gabriel Druillettes which documented the seventeenth-century history of the river. We contacted local experts in both archaeology and historic preservation, as well as the Penobscot tribe for rules regarding Native burials. In this process, we were told a story of the building of a small chapel just across from the parcel we were on. In this story, a priest had documented that upon leaving the chapel by its back door, he had observed the presence of three wooden crosses on the land across the river. The crosses, he stated, had been erected on the graves of the children of a Native man.

Our first trip back to the site was a happy one, for we came bearing gifts. Late the previous fall, we had journeyed to the children to see if there was anything they needed. When a late fall fair opened, we searched all the craft booths for the requested items: a small double hand drum dressed in yellow and red, and a hand-carved model of an esteemed Native friend, the beloved May-May. We found a stone box

---

* We experienced the vigilant protectiveness of the Little People only early on. Initially, we were concerned about a manipulative or harmful presence, but this feeling and experience ended when our relationship with the area deepened.

with a slide-away cover and stored the toys there, such that on a sunny day we could remove the top and feel the children's joy.

As time passed, our feelings and thoughts about the children's presence matured. We came to have knowledge of their individual characters and reactions. We came to love their play and their trust that we would not hurt them. We were happy they had found us but wondered what it was that their souls might have done if time had not stopped for them those many years before. With my own history, I could not pretend to be restricted to one lifetime: How could I wish differently for them? I began to wonder what had held them there, and what their people had believed. We hoped they had passed nonviolently. If disease had claimed them it would have been tragic, but we were not blinded to the fact that it could have been worse. Katetin was joyful and bright, quiet and brave. The younger boy touched my soul. He reminded me of the small boy I had searched for so often in my repetitive childhood dream. The coincidence of our contact and my soul's purpose was too much to ignore. We decided to pursue answers shamanically to help fill in the pieces our research had remained silent on. What had happened on the river, and what role had the children played? Only if we could understand that could we decide if something could be done or should be done to move them forward. At the same time, I knew I had to dig deeper into my own motivation for the search. Remembering the lessons of that Native man I had been, I sensed there would be a time when ego had to fall away. It would be too easy to step into their story and fall victim to blame and hatred. That would be a clear violation of that set of original instructions. After contacting a trusted teacher, I reentered shamanic group work on the Healing of Place. Determined to be able to speak transparently, I knew I would have to discover more about that battle in my own past. Only then would I know where my limits with these two children must be.

In shamanic journeying, work of the spirit is sacred, between the person who travels and those in Spirit who may agree to help. The traveler seldom goes alone, and he or she engages allies to find answers and set limits to contact. In order to have the clearest, most untainted view of the answers, the traveler will have issues of their own come up, and these must be addressed. In this work, there were several participants led by more experienced practitioners, to maintain safety and provide structure for the rest of us. We were tasked to find an ancestor in Spirit to help with the Healing of Place and make contact with a Guardian of the Land.

Over the course of the next several months, the work was approached with three purposes. One was to learn the histories of each participant's parcel of land. Each participant was a shamanic practitioner in his or her own right. Each would have experienced injury and disturbance on their chosen piece of land and would have asked the Land if it required assistance in healing. All would have received permission to do such work. Another purpose was to develop relationship with my own extended past and get an idea as to why I might have been called to involve myself with this place. The third was to use this knowledge and intent to change the energy of what may have happened and, in my case, to release the children, if that was what was needed.

*I, Linda, am a creature of the night, the deep times, the spirit hours.
I love the dark journeys best. I lie draped across the damp moss, which
smells like grit and tastes of green. I feel the cool light of the gibbous
moon across my skin. Slowly, the coolness pools until I am a puddle of
light, rolling in a viscous mass into the midst of the rounded stones.
Musk and mud and the tangy bite of wild onion.*

*I slide into the River's welcome, feel her arms wrap about me
in long, ropy caresses. My belly fur rubs the bottom. I am Otter, and
I roll and tumble toward the sound which pulls me upriver. Bubbles clink and pop as they push past me, like glass as they reflect the
light above. Some get trapped by my whiskered face and then I am
the mighty sturgeon, leaping clear of the River's arms to touch my
snout to the moon's bright glow. Crashing down, I land on eight
running legs and crayfish scuttles into shadow. Then I am Eel,
beneath the shadow of the stones. I feel the bubbles pass and the
River's arms break into waves upon the dark rocks. Just before I
land, I am the Water itself, with its round presence and ancient
memory. My inner eye gives me a picture of a land unseen and far
away, the water's journey into the here and now. I am Otter once
again, lying along a sunken log. I have the moonlight in my tight,
small ears.*

*As my eyes empty of light, I see the Shapechanger, the guardian
with many faces. An eagle's head dives down, trailed by a long mane
of cloud; then it is a deer's graceful neck and sweep of antler. Its nose
gently reaches out to touch my furred face and I ask, "What is the
name of this song, the story of this Place? What is the memory that
the stones hold?"*

The Guardian pulls back, its shape formed only by the light of the moon's soft rays. The stones begin to shift and mumble: Who will tell the story? Their voices are a rumble and a clatter as two among them slide lower. From beneath, a craggy rock appears.

"I have the memory," it says. "A liquid story which started as a drop of warmth upon my face. The drop was warm and tasted of the sea, strange upon my stone face." I listened for what seemed a moment: The moss people came and covered the drop. Then it was the moss, the drop, and me. And the drop became my face and it sang a single note. Finally, it began to speak.

"And once the memory came upon me," said the Stone, "brought into time by the Water in that single drop, I had its story. In my own slow way, I spoke to my neighbors, who turned and rolled, rumbled and shifted. The bits of moss tumbled into the cracks and roots, and mycelia carried the moss into the spaces between wet stones. Memory was shared and rugged faces formed, wise faces who perhaps had appeared among the two-leggeds, ancestors of the child who had rested above.

"In unusual hurry the message passed up the hill, shivering through the aspen and rolling the stone people beneath. There was a brief pause as the moss people hesitated at the edge of the sunnier meadow. Going underground again, all the relations, moss, root, and stone, formed support for the lone man above. Hunkered on his heels, now bowed with age, the child's father dropped tears among them. And as it had before, the memory was passed back to my stone face to be stored for time unmeasured."

"Can you take me there?" The otter's whiskered face touched the stone's surface.

This time the stone remained silent. Its face rolled upward, thrusting its neighbors in the same direction. I landed my clawed feet among their flattened faces, and leapt up the waterfall's course, feeling my way along the traces of memory I saw and felt as we traveled upwards. Then he was there, as he must have been in the days that followed the battle, elbows on his thighs and shoulders dropped. Katetin's father squatted there, his posture echoing helplessness, pain, and disbelief. I stood behind him for a long time, once again a human observer of his grief. I had no touch to share, only the memory of a similar loss. All I could offer was a promise to help the Land to heal.

AE

Through all our journeys, we learned that the Land was healing; that it had been deeply affected by violence occurring upon it. It wondered if my family intended more violence. Were we only the next occupying army? It was willing to contract with us to continue the work together so long as we realized what our lifetime looked like to the stones and trees. We were told that our lives of self-importance were like gnats on the face of a mountain; that in order to stop the pain of its injury, the Land had stopped its time; that the energy of that violence would have continued to ripple across the vibration of Creation long after our short lives were done. Healing could be assisted by changing the energy there. It had experienced great harm; but its healing could be hastened and intensified by ceremony, which was described in some detail. The Land gave us the story of the children's fate, their bravery and persistence in the face of their separation from their parents. It was that sacrifice that had snagged the attention of Spirit. To help heal this, we were to create a monument to their sacrifice so that all could approach a place of respect and remembrance. We were to pursue peace between the Red and White People who had interacted here, in such a way that that would discourage violence from ever happening again. Spirit described a process and ceremony to free the children to their families, such that their presence was voluntary. If we were successful, we were to place upon the monument the handprints of Two Peoples in paint created from the Land, to remind others of the bond between us.

It was required of me to confront the shadow self, the events which might bind me to ego and memory and cause the work here to fail. I was reminded that I was here to serve as a bridge between Peoples, and for that purpose only had I been allowed to retain memory of past lives. Not to be special and therefore apart, but to use the preparation given to serve that which was greater. The Land itself was to be preserved as a testament to such.

We started with the monument, looking at artists' work throughout the late summer and fall. Although many were beautiful, none seemed to express what Spirit intended. Finally, as fall turned the sanctuary a million hues of color, we found a granite monolith six feet tall; too tall to be sat upon but approachable in all its aspects. The shape was subtly female, seeming to enclose in its silvery arms the shapes of two children, one taller than the other. Within two weeks, it had traveled to the meadow site and was set within view of all three mounds. Slowly it was righted and sunk several inches into the soil and sand. A stone fountain joined it and was kept filled with water, to offer its coolness to the wild relations. A planting was made of native plants and the children's toy box added.

Just before the stone was set, the last of our group's meetings occurred. Each of us had spent a summer journeying to our injured places, being told elements of what had happened there, and being given instruction on how to assist in healing. Together the group journeyed to each place, each person experiencing their own perspective on the Land's injury and needs. Each participant had a piece of the mosaic. In my case, the leaders found the children first. Their individual accounts confirmed our own vision about their ages and personalities. No longer afraid, our love and commitment had already begun a process of healing the racial trauma. With love they were taken to their mother, for whom they had been waiting. I remained with their father, witnessing his grief at the loss of his entire family. One peer was taken to a Scottish woman who had remained behind to care for the children. Another was introduced to the Guardian of this place and was allowed to play with animal spirits there. It was as if we all had positions on the same stage, experiencing some elements of the place's history in common, while receiving individual guidance. Together the experiences created a picture of place in three dimensions, or in many. And all across an enormous span of time. Ceremony occurred to the specification of Spirit. The children were taken to their mother, who received them with joyous smiles and arms opened wide. We were told they would be allowed to play still, as they desired, on their road to whatever destiny awaited them. We asked about their infant brother and were told that the child had passed quickly, too new to hold back and gone with its mother. My heart turned to the children's father, so reticent in making contact, but of him there was no longer any sign. I remembered my own dream search for a son not found, and felt sadness and determination to bring him peace if it was needed.

And so the stones were set in the fall. The morning air was misty, raindrops from the previous day clinging to leaf and vine. Henry and I stood at the anticipated spot to guide the Caterpillar in with its central stone pylon. The Native children were present, and the dog barked with the growling of the big machine. The children sensed our joy and emotion, but were afraid of the noise of the machine's approach. I felt them retreat down the path but went to fetch them, reminding them that this growling animal brought a forever reminder of their bravery and their mother's love. Didn't they want to see? So they remained a safe distance behind us, as the stone and fountain were placed. As the machine retreated we felt their mother join us, her round fullness and joy enveloping us all as she marshalled the children to surround the granite monolith, so like a mother with children in arms. As Henry and I joined hands, we felt the approach of a different energy. It was more defined, and definitely male. I remained still, afraid acknowledgment would be inappropriate. And with three bold steps he joined us, his height and breadth of shoulder identifying him immediately. Slowly, Katetin's father placed a quiet hand on each of our shoulders. For mere moments, time stopped. We were all together; four parents joined in the love of two children. We felt his quiet approval, a sense of his smile and her joy. Then the children smiled as well, and in a minute they were gone, the father passing behind us to sweep his beloved ones away.

●

The work has continued in the several years since the events in this story occurred. In subtle ways, the Land has become more inspirited. Plant species we have discussed adding but just wished for occasionally appear on their own, popping up like surprise relations at the door. We are sometimes joined by the Presence of an older Native man, who especially appears when we are teaching youth or children. I think he listens to what we are passing on to the children of the future. An older martial arts student meets him in the pathway sometimes, and sometimes we feel him at the door. In 2015 the site was shared for a weekend staff retreat by Maine-Wabanaki REACH, meeting for the purpose of Truth and Reconciliation, joining forces on a path to move into a better future, which made our hearts sing. At the end of the meeting, a rehabilitated young eagle was released back onto the Kennebec. The crate was held by a team of Native Penobscot women on one side and Avian Haven volunteers and staff on the other. The young female bird erupting into the air between the two seemed to carry with it a prayer for the future, maybe a message to Spirit that a new time was coming. It certainly was a living testament to the power of hope and healing. From inside the pale shell of this body, my soul rose with it.

Epilogue

The day had boiled up warm and humid outside the yurt on the river. Menacing clouds had piled up on themselves on the western horizon, overtaking each other and jostling their fellows as they grumbled along toward the water. Just before our martial arts class began, they broke upon the hillside and the wind rose to a howl. I closed the glass doors, listening to the children's parents as they adjusted a uniform or reminded each child again to listen in class. It was graduation day. My youngest student, a girl about Katetin's age, would not be able to join us. I would miss her spirit and spunk, but turned my attention to the two boys who currently trained with us. Now closing in on eleven, they rushed in at the last moment, active attention on the snack table and the excitement of a new belt. The first few minutes of congratulations were nearly drowned out by the roar of the storm sweeping over the skylight.

As the ceremony of belt tying occurred, the audience became solemn and their new tasks were explained. As it does for all young warriors, the subject turned to the nature of heroism. Several people gave examples from stories, television, and a few from life events. One parent mentioned that warriorhood was confusing in the world today, and wondered what it looked like for the generation to come. We began a discussion about where the children would find community, with many families separated by hundreds of miles. For several very important years, these families had grown with ours, working at the school's yurt, growing food together, laughing and sometimes trading work for lessons. One boy wondered if a girl could be a warrior too, worried about his younger sister being left out. We told them that warriorhood starts by making sure that the actions one takes are the same whether someone sees them or not; and we reminded them to consider other beings in the communities that surrounded them, regardless of where that was. So saying, we handed one boy a small plate of food to be placed at the monument for all our Relations. When he returned, both boys asked if there was something *they* could give back to honor warrior spirit. I thought about the question and how to make a demonstration of respect meaningful to two young boys, something they might not forget as the years bore them forward. Long ago I had woven elements of Katetin's story into their training, always cushioning them from the truth behind the lesson. As Henry threw open the back door, the storm moved east, and a rainbow lit the back of the retreating tumult. I gathered the boys close then and told them of Katetin's great courage and the cost to her and her family. Would they like to demonstrate what they had learned as tribute to one so brave? Indeed, they would.

So in bare feet we picked our way through the rain-soaked grass, the sky overhead lit by the colors of the rainbow. They solemnly lined themselves up just beyond the monument. We faced the eastern sky and together dropped into a deep bow. I asked them to think of Katetin as they began the rhythmic movements of their forms, and I followed suit. As we all ended together, we drew ourselves to full height and bowed again, our hearts searching for a small girl who had shown tremendous courage.

It was as we rose that I saw her in the middle of the path, the great oak behind her, streamers of evening sun passing through and around her. Her face was a solemn study, her eyes large and her hair moving gently in the wind. Her face was no longer a child's face, but that of a young woman. As the boys rose and stood facing her, it was as if I watched the scene from another perspective. Her hand raised, palm toward us, and then she was gone.

I don't think the boys saw her, but the moments following were uncharacteristically quiet. There was no customary race back to their families, perhaps sensing a time that would not come again. Following goodbyes all around, the grounds stilled and night chased them back onto the road and into the world. Darkness dropped over the meadow on the hill. Fireflies lit up the night within moments, and the frogs in the pond began a sonorous rumble as the world began another turn.

And so the children are at peace. We feel them close to us on occasion, but with none of the urgency of previous times. Katetin brushes past my body, her presence a warm wind against my earthbound flesh, using her energy for her own resources. We are told the Land no longer requires active protection, but we steward it carefully in our ideas for the future. This year we are going deep within, furthering relationship and seeking ways to slowly make human presence reciprocal with the Land.

As I write this, I realize that words on paper do not capture what we have felt about these children. If I tell you a story with my mouth, I am counting on my gestures, the emotion in my eyes, the wonder and humility, the catch of my throat in order for you to see. The writing of this tells you the doing of it, not the effect on my soul.

What did my heart do as I held the essence of Katetin in my arms at that fall campfire, now years gone? Was it the turning of her small head in trust against my shoulder, or the wind? Was that the smell of warmth as she shifted; or the feel of her hand's tiny bones against my palm? My words have told you the doing of our time together, but I struggle to find words for the being of it.

When I think about that monument on the hill, my heart and eyes fill, and something larger than my body can feel the shape of the time her parents lost with her, can sense like my own skin her inward deter-mination and composure, and still I will fail to bring you the joy of her.

It's a soul thing, you see. If you had a chair by that fire, you might not have seen her. Or maybe a part of you would. The memory of her hair smelled of child and campfire, and as she shifted, her skin smelled of warm earth and sun and my inner eye made her shoulder round against the firelight. People would say she was not there that night, how could she have been in the same time and space I was in? And yet she was. I know her still. My heart paints her picture against the curve of my eye. "Good imagination," you say.

Only Time knows. But in every way that matters, Katetin is still alive. Her essential being, like yours or mine, has no color or gender and has not been erased. She is memory and starlight. Maybe she has come again into the world. When all of us meet each other's eyes as strangers, perhaps we will see her. Native people once said that their White younger brothers and sisters could either come as trusted friends or as destroyers. It was said that this time might come again, and some say this time is here right now. What will we be to the Grandchildren this time? What will Katetin see now?

The final illustration does not try to represent Katetin's freed Spirit. Only she can create that and I do not presume to portray it. Rather, it is a reminder that any gratitude we feel for the present should lead to change in the future. Grief experienced fully for past actions must result in changes in those actions to consider all Relations in the future. Perhaps this is the meaning of atonement—at-one-ment—or the moment we all realize we are the same. What we do to others, we do to ourselves.

Afterword

As stated in the introduction, the autobiographical material and verifiable events in this story are true. The presence of Native persons in this area of the river is based on their statements; there is also archaeological evidence of occupation for a very long period of time, including the story's time. History has left us trail markers from the perspective of the settlers and missionaries. They made contact with a Native man in our area in years following this possible scenario. He spoke to them about the death of his children and their gravesite near the river.

Much of Katetin's story must remain a mystery. Even her name and Instip's are common Eastern Abenaki names, as that is my best understanding of what would have been their tribal affiliation at the time cited. They would have been part of the Wabanaki confederacy. The western side of the Kennebec River was never ceded by them in intent and remained a demarcation line between first tribal societies and then the Native and British. The warfare between the British and Natives, including the massacre at Norridgewock (Narantsouak), would become so terrible that for over fifty years the British would not return to our portion of the Kennebec. This is borne out by research and by landmarks like cemetery dates along the West River Road in Augusta and Sidney. Most of the Abenaki survivors of the massacre in 1724 either made their way to the Penobscots farther north, or retreated to Canada—specifically Quebec (Kebik), where their descendants live today. My children's ancestors were among them. Some families remain in areas of northwestern Maine.

In this writing, events among early colonists and the battle scene near our location are based on composite evidence which had begun to occur in the early seventeenth century, historical tensions and trends in trade at the time. The specifics of the battle itself were the result of shamanic experience of one of my dear mentors, Dr. Chris Marshall. Dr. Marshall has generously given his permission for this wording. His view of the battle lines flowing across the cliff face follows me still.

For people who might wonder what became of my dad, he went on to become a well-known artist within his own niche. It would be exaggerating to say that his life ever became simple, but he received well-deserved respect for the work he did and was an example to many outside our family. He and my mother remained together until his passing, and when they left the house in Maine, things got much better. Things he said over the course of years made me wonder if Spirit perhaps considered him for a role in reconciliation at some point. He chose reading material for us early on that reflected a great respect for Native people. He was sensitive and aware of some of the larger issues, shared many of the same practices and connections to our Wild Relations, and seemed himself born outside his own time. War had run him over, had taken his sensitivity and warped it into something foreign to his nature. He was more peaceful in later years, and we were all close when he passed.

During the years Katetin was with us, the inner warrior inside me was brought to the forefront. It was important to weigh a series of innate responses which arose as knowledge of the children's fate and the consideration of their possible futures arose. Early on in personal work, a shamanic guide acting as psychopomp (spirit guide, Chris Marshall) met with my dream self and heard the grief and pain of a young war chief. Guising himself as an old clan mother, he bore the anger of lost fatherhood onward and allowed the spirit of the young man to begin to heal. The reader may be pleased to know that his missing child has made his way again into this world, allowing his parenting to be completed. The relationship of the young warrior to a precious guide who "came along" to help was also explained. People who know the story have different interpretations about the nature of this relationship.

I have increasingly noted a lifelong relationship with the Hudson River. When I was a child, my parents would drive along its length, and I remember the sensation of longing and great weight when passing the Catskills. Without exception, there would be the temptation to leave the car and go "home." Realizing such action would cause a grievous response, I gradually forgot about it after making Maine my home as an adult. It was an oddity without context. During the Katetin years, I cared for a relative in my state of origin, and again had cause to notice it. During one such trip, we camped at a historic battle site outside Albany. At this site of Native and British conflict, I was made aware that the woods around the site were populated by the soft outlines of Native people who quietly walked among the trees. They seemed to go about their tasks mostly unaware of my regard. They made me feel peaceful, as if I was no longer alone on the landscape. That night, I once again had the Native past-life dream, this time seeming to travel from my tent site through the woods as if carried by the wind. The silhouette of the mountains passed quickly, and I entered a familiar valley from the north. As the familiar but traumatic attack began to play itself out, I withdrew quietly from the scene. When I woke, I told Henry it was time for the war chief to go home. With a mild feeling of foolishness layered on grim determination, I drove us onto Route 87 and headed south along the west bank of the Hudson. For the better part of an hour, we traveled with no set goal. Shortly afterward, a feeling of unease settled upon me, followed by a heavy sense of loss and the sensation of having been torn from some vital part of self. In a bizarre way, I also felt great joy at approaching what my inner self knew as "home." With tears threatening to overcome good driving sense,

I rolled into a service exit, threw open the car door, and fell to my knees in the grass and sand. Looking up, I saw a worn and rust-encrusted historical marker, marking the site of the Esopus Wars of the 1650s.

Two distinct conflicts had occurred here, with the son of the local peace chief killed during the first conflict. The area had been settled originally by descendants of the Lenni Lenape tribe, who had moved along the great river for hundreds of years. Here the tribe had subdivided into smaller groups in distinct areas along the lower, middle, and upper mountains and valley. The area was colonized by the Dutch in early contact years, who were eventually replaced by the British from the southeast. The number of settlers had become an alarming flood; earlier cooperation was replaced with a press for resources and land. Because of this, the newer settlements maintained a distinctly military presence; and as the boundary frayed and the river became a superhighway, the small Dutch settlement became a walled town, defending its growth from an increasingly threatened population of Native people. Because of the military presence, meticulous records of the conflicts survive to this day. Over two days, I read through these accounts, noting casually the names of combatants and following a battle I had watched and acted out since early childhood. I felt anger and sadness rise and determined that they did not serve a larger purpose. I felt sadness and shame at reading about the local peace chief, who had loved his powerful sons but fought in vain to prevent the destruction of his lifeways. (I have come to know this man as my peacekeeper, who identified himself to me in hypnosis as "Petiseyawan," which in Lenni Lenape means "He who comes along.")

Final accounts placed him in a small shanty many years later, having bartered for simple survival until few of the People remained. I made the decision to disregard names and places, although they were recorded. They were an attachment to ego which did not lead to ease. Instead I gave the chief's son a nickname from the Land and we conducted ceremony to honor the People.

On our last day, we decided to walk about the old part of town. I had visited the area at the foot of the mountains and made some attempt to locate the relative position of some of the old village sites. Preferring not to dwell, we wanted to see if we could get a feel from the old town's character. At the very center, we found the site of the original Dutch fort, with a monument and perimeter lined with grass and trees. The history of the battles had made a point of mentioning that the center of the town had never been breached by Native forces. I recalled this as I stood just beyond the area. I felt an unusual hesitation, studying my own toes positioned just outside the line. Feeling a combination of sadness, pride, and justice, I stepped slowly into the center and up to the monument. I wondered how the history would be presented. I saw the usual story of conflict and misunderstanding, of limits and boundaries. Someone, most likely a Native visitor, had carefully crossed out a line on the tablet and left a soft turkey feather as a gifting beneath the edge of the marble. I laid my hand upon it, again musing on the warrior inside the pale skin. I remembered that moment many times after, and again when I received a final teaching in March 2017 from the Peacekeeper who came with me. During that time, I was caused to understand the price of peace; the willingness to do anything to preserve life at the moment of extinction; to barter pride and self-worth for the future and the Grandchildren. For the first time in my life, I surrendered my separation from the past and present and felt both shattered and whole. I suspect the warrior inside will never disappear completely, but he has finally found wisdom to replace knowledge in the role of the Peacekeeper.

The Best Friend I Never Met

William Eagle, Bill, was already quite ill when he became a part of my life in an official capacity. As part of my job, I was to determine if I could help him, applying some objective and stringent rules. Because I knew how ill he was, I worked hard to rise above strict requirements to make things happen quickly for him.

He called to thank me. I replied it was my job.

He told me it was my job to be objective, which he appreciated, but not necessarily to be kind. He asked how he could thank me in a personal way, to return the kindness. I said he could not.

Bill hung up and called a secretary and got the agency's address. He sent a small, handmade token for me. I told him I could not accept it, could not be singled out or made "special." He said I already was.

I spoke to a supervisor, who confirmed that no one could be singled out unless everyone was. Bill asked how many people did what I did, to which I replied, "About seventy." He then sent seventy small tokens, handmade. It became a joke at work, whimsical and unheard of. He kept occasionally calling, and more items followed, always in batches of seventy. He would ask how I was and I would tell him small, recent events.

When my husband left our family, I couldn't speak at all, even about small events. Knowing how little family I had, the agency agreed it was okay to give Bill my contact information. He would call and I would just listen to the stories he told, about his home in North Carolina and his beloved Mountains, about riding rodeo as a younger man. We spoke about the personal loss he felt being away from the Land in his Blood and the memories he had about being raised in a Cherokee family. We

· 85 ·

talked about the beauty of his Native beliefs and the grief of the losses they had incurred. His tone always remained peaceful, while I spouted anger and outrage at their treatment. When I stopped speaking, he said, "Oh, Little One, you may be White on the outside, but you are Red on the inside." Hearing this statement raised by someone outside myself shocked me into anger. How many times in the last year had people told me they knew how I felt? How many ways could I be afraid for my children? "You don't know anything about who I am," I raged. "You don't even know me!"

"I'm afraid I do," he said gently.

Bill told me about the Rainbow Warriors. The stories varied depending to some degree on where they originated. He believed that in some way, the souls of his people might come through again when the world was ready for their wisdom. From that time on, he treated me like the tenderest of wild creatures. For some years, he called me at home to check on the children, whom he called "Rainbow Kids." He hand-knitted socks for them in winter and spoke gently to them on the phone. I'd walk by and hear his soft southern drawl as he gave them advice, sang, or told them a story. He desperately regretted his estrangement from his own children. He would call and share his grief after an unsuccessful attempt at contact with them, and then pour the love he had into mine.

As the years went by, he continued to send occasional gifts to the people at my workplace when he could find seventy of any small item. He became a fixture in our lives and only once again brought up my importance in his eyes, as a bridge between our two peoples. He told outrageous stories about calling in Moose and then riding Him around. I was *almost* sure he was kidding. The week came when he didn't call, and then another passed. What should I do, what if something was wrong? Maybe he had just moved on with his life or said all he had to say…then I found his obituary. I wished I could offer my sympathy to his family but knew I had to respect their privacy. I have quietly sent them prayers and continue to do so. Two years ago, Henry and I traveled to his beloved Mountains, and we stopped by the road and threw tobacco into the wind, imagining him home along with us. His quiet belief in what I represented to him had given him happiness and me invaluable support. You see, I never got to see his face in person.

He was the best friend I never met. **LRH**

Background Reading

The following is a wide list based on material from which I extracted information, included in the "Portent" and "Rarefaction" sections of this book. The list is not exhaustive, as ideas were pulled in a general way from over a decade of research into the history of Native people in Maine.

Above the Gravel Bar: The Native Canoe Routes of Maine, by David S. Cook. 3rd Edition: Polar Bear and Company, Solon, Maine, 2007.

The Centennial History of Waterville, Kennebec County Maine, by Rev. Edwin Carey Whittemore. Published by the Executive Committee of the Centennial Celebration, 1902.

Dawn over the Kennebec, by Mary C. Calvert. Twin City Printery, Lewiston, Maine, 1986.

"Father Sebastian Rasle and the Indian Massacre at Narrantsauak [Norridgewock]" by Nowetah Cyr. Nowetah's American Indian Museum, New Portland, Maine.

"Earthfast Architecture in Early Maine," a paper presented by Emerson Baker, et al., at the Vernacular Architecture Forum annual meeting, Portsmouth, New Hampshire, 1992. On the website of Virtual Norumbega—The Northern New England Frontier: http://w3.salemstate.edu/~ebaker/earthfast/earthfastpaper.html.

"Exhibit highlights artillery collection at Fort Ticonderoga," by Chris Carola, Associated Press. In *Seattle Times*, May 30, 2016.

"Horse Raising in Colonial New England," by Deane Phillips. Memoir 54. Cornell University Agricultural Experiment Station. Ithaca, New York, 1922.

Illustrated History of Kennebec County Maine, edited by Henry D. Kingsbury and Simeon L. Deyo. H.W. Blake & Co., New York, 1892.

Indian Antiquities of the Kennebec Valley, by Charles C. Willoughby. Published by The Maine Historic Preservation Commission and the Maine State Museum, Augusta, Maine, 1980.

The Jesuit Relations and Allied Documents: Travels and Explorations of the Jesuit Missionaries in New France 1610–1791, Volume XXXVI, edited by Ruben Gold Thwaites, et al. The Burrows Brothers Company, Cleveland, 1898.

"The Kennebec," in *Maine Catholic Historical Magazine*, 1914.

The Mortification of Sin in Believers: Containing the Necessity, Nature and Means of It with a Resolution of Sundry Cases of Conscience Thereunto Belonging, by John Owen, D.D. Nathanael Ponder, pub., London, 1668.

"Ne-Do-Ba (Friends): Exploring and Sharing the Wabanaki History of Interior New England." Website: www.nedoba.org.

The Old Maps of Kennebec County, Maine in 1879, compiled by Caldwell & Halfpenny. The Write Stuff Graphic Design and Printing, Fryeburg, Maine.

Norumbega Reconsidered: Mawooshen and the Wawenoc Diaspora, by H.G. Brack. Pennywheel Press, Hulls Cove, Maine, 2008.

Notes on a Lost Flute: A Field Guide to the Wabanaki, by Kerry Hardy. Down East Books, Camden, Maine, 2009.

"Upstate NY fort with long history offers new ways to view it," by Chris Carola. Associated Press News, June 20, 2016.

The Wabanakis of Maine and the Maritimes, by The American Friends Service Committee. Maine Indian Program of the New England Regional Office of the American Friends Service Committee, 1989.

Credit here is also given to author Susan Power, from her novel *The Grass Dancer* (Berkley Books, 1995). Her description of the moon being a palpable presence both inside and outside the body is one that I had experienced, but had no words or precedent to follow. In this reference, the moon is where souls come and go from—and so exists in two places or in many at the same time. And for further reading in shamanic healing, I suggest Llyn Roberts's book *Shamanic Reiki: Expanded Ways of Working with Universal Life Force Energy* (Moon Books, 2007).

Notes on Terms and Places

Black Robe – A Black Robe or Blackrobe was a Roman Catholic priest. Prevalent in the Americas, Black Robes were named so for their long black cassocks. Those present in the Northeast were often French Jesuits. Their original mission was the conversion of the Native people. Father Rasle of Norridgewock (anglicized) actively defended his assigned Native families from British incursion and was murdered with them in 1724.

Clout – An old-fashioned expression meaning diaper; multilayered infant covering.

Cushnoc or **C/Koussinok** – Anglicized word for a Wabanaki phrase for "head of tide" in some records, or "sacred place" in others. Also, the early settlement, trading center, and later fort between Hallowell and current-day Augusta, Maine. This is also the old name for the trading site which first appeared at the confluence of what is now Route 17 or Eastern Avenue and Arsenal Street by the Kennebec River.

Earthfast building – An architectural technique common in the early contact period: a post-in-ground technique where posts were placed in holes or on sills without foundation. There is discussion on whether these were intended as semipermanent structures. They were more frequent on the coast than in the interior.

"First Blood" refers to "virgin soil" epidemics, those which came about by direct and indirect contact with European people. Indigenous people here had no immunologic defense from these diseases and so were devastated by them.

Gluscabe-glue-skaw-buh (Abenaki) – Northeastern cultural hero Abenaki, Wabanaki. Spoken of as "First Man" in some stories, born directly of Creator.

Green Beings – "Standing still" or green plant relatives. Considered as people in community with, and healers of, other relations (four-leggeds, two-leggeds, winged ones, etc.). "Standing Still People" are described and thought of among Indigenous people as their own Nation or Tribe of equal relations. This is true for many shamanic practitioners, both Native and non-Native. There exists an alliance, a deep relationship, between the healer, the plant, and the client in an agreement to heal.

Guardian of the Land – See Shapechanger.

Highland Games – Many states have Clan Gatherings, cultural gatherings of Celtic and Scottish people who came to live in this country. While probably initiated mainly for trade and reunion, these large gatherings feature many different clans or families, all of whom compete in athletic competition as well as dance and living culture.

Kebik – Quebec. This word has various spellings.

Land of the Grandfathers – It is said among some that the most ancient roots of the Algonquin people were found in the Lenni Lenape, historically the people of the eastern coasts of New Jersey, New York, and eastern Pennsylvania. Dutch history speaks of the Hudson tribe's disappearance in great numbers, both through direct contact and through indirect contact with livestock, traders, etc. Historians painted a picture of camps eerily still, meals untouched, and personal items lying where they fell—as if just dropped from a human hand.

Little People – Little People are comparable to the Fey in Celtic and other societies. They can be described as guardians of the Land they hold, mischievous, and also protective of the Land overall.

May-May – A cultural myth or story about how the pileated woodpecker earned its red hair; it is a story of loyalty and friendship.

Medawlinno – Eastern Abenaki for medicine person, or shaman (east-Asian/North-Asian term). This "speaking breath" is a reference to a specific cultural practice associated with a shaman and his plant allies in the matter of awakening their medicine. Source: www.nedoba.org.

Mejachkawit is a historical Abenaki figure who appears in history in the mid-1630s and became associated with Father Gabriel Druillettes. The Chapel of the Assumption across from us was built in the mid-1640s, although quite a bit of ambassadorial work by Mejachkawit is intimated previously by several sources, among which is Mary Calvert's *Dawn over the Kennebec*. This site was located across the river from our land, near the current Cives Steel Company (Augusta).

Narantsouak and **Narrantsauak** are two spellings used in the early years for the village known today by the anglicized name Norridgewock.

Portent – A foreshadowing or sign. In this case, a series of smaller events and changes, the significance of which is not yet clear to either Katetin's family or the settlers in the area.

Psychopomp is the term for a person who assists the souls of the dead. This assistance includes being a guide for the soul not traveling beyond, and may include providing information or healing services. Famous psychopomps include Anubis (Egypt) and Hermes (Greek). The job is to escort, explain, and walk beside.

"Rain on Dust," a phrase I use in this book, is meant to imply a momentous settling, a falling into place, a sort of life affirmation of purpose, which finding Katetin had for me. But it is also a phrase used as a book title by a Teacher of my Teacher, Martin Prechtel. In his book, *The Smell of Rain on Dust*, Mr. Prechtel describes the effect of trauma and grief which murder and death inscribe on the human soul. The book describes the impact of violence which both I and the Land felt and which requires healing.

Rainbow Warrior – The prophetic belief held by Native Nations that there would be a time when all people would stand at a crossroads where it was required to choose between greed and reconciliation with Earth Mother. If all joined in changing their ways, a new time of prosperity would come. The messengers of this change were spoken of as Rainbow Warriors, and they were said to pave the way for the return of wise ancestors with old teachings to lead the way.

Rarefaction is a term common to geology, physics, metaphysics, music, and mathematics. In strictest terms, it is the impact point where energy ripples in waves, then turns and comes back to center, crossing over its own lines. This concept appears in the story as a collision in ripples of time. On our land, we have frequently heard singing down by the cliff's edge, as well as accompaniment to our drumming. It is easy to picture a confluence in the echoes of Time; a feeling that Spirit has entry there and that the physical present exists alongside it.

Reiki energy is a high-frequency healing form of Universal energy. The practitioner is not the Source of this energy, but a conduit, or a "hollow bone" in shamanic terms. When combined with shamanic practice, Reiki can be used to heal the soul outside of normal time constraints. Per Llyn Roberts in her book *Shamanic Reiki*, "Shamanic work happens in the realm of soul. Therefore, a soul in transition can be healed before life or after death." This is the work of the psychopomp (see above).

Restoration, referred to in text as "restored areas" – We (Henry and I) have spent eleven years engaged in the process of not only returning the land on the Kennebec to what it may have looked like prior to First Contact, but also making it a medicinal plant sanctuary. We do this by encouraging wild medicinals to grow where they are most happy locally, and by supplementing them with a variety of mostly native regional medicinals. The plantings occur at ground level, at woody shrub level, and finally at canopy level. The effect is a shallow layer of plants numerically, but a very wide variety of species by type. We are working with Indigenous people to return this space to its essence as a protected, sacred, and educational place.

Ring-pin – A common Native North American children's game, where a ring of variable materials is tossed in the air and must be speared by the pin. For more information: www.beyondthechalkboard.org/activity/ring-and-pin/

Shapechanger – In this book, the Shapechanger is variously known as Spirit of Place, Wind Spirit, or Guardian of the Land.

Sillery – A town absorbed into what became the city of Quebec. It became a haven in early historical times for Jesuit priests and their Indigenous converts. The French perspective sees Maine as settled from the north southward rather than from the south of New England northward.

Wind Spirit – See Shapechanger.

CPSIA information can be obtained
at www.ICGtesting.com
Printed in the USA
LVHW010228280821
696293LV00006B/1175